I am excited about what I experienced while reading this healing journey. As I read with vigor (I couldn't put the book down), I discovered so many facets of the revelation of Christ as healer, physician, faithful friend, lawyer, confidant, miracle worker, and comforter. As I read I was drawn closer to God. What a life-changing journey!

—LUIDA JOHNSON, FOUNDING PASTOR
SHABACH FOURSQUARE CHURCH

This is a great series that will bless many. I'm sure that boys and girls all over will enjoy reading as much as I have. I can see it being put into a movie. Thank you for the privilege of reviewing this great work.

—DORCAS McREYNOLDS, MASTER TEACHER

Scars: An emotional Injury more painful than ones you can see with your eyes. Davida harbored so many throughout her young life: disappointments, abuse at the hand of a date, a father who was not there for her and a mother who weathered her own storms.

Read this powerful novel and learn just how Davida managed to make hers disappear. I feel honored to have been asked to read and review this outstanding novel.

This book gets FIVE GOLDEN STARS AND FIVE GOLDEN SUNLIGHTS TO BLOCK OUT THE STORM CLOUDS!

—FRAN LEWIS, BOOK REVIEWER

I would say, "Yes," you certainly accomplished what you set out to do!!! You did it fabulously!!!! Wonderful chapters. Superb ending.

—JOY WASSEL, PhD, PROFESSIONAL COUNSELOR

This is a well-written interesting memoire. I always enjoy and totally relate to your writing. Thank you for the honor.

—ADDIE K. BURROUGHS, HIGH SCHOOL TEACHER

The Garbage Man's Daughter

Book 4

Letting
Go
of
Scars

GLORIA SHELL MITCHELL

EncourageMint
Books

Gardena, CA

ISBN-13: 978-0-9761010-5-5
ISBN-10: 0-9761010-5-X

Library of Congress Control Number: 2010939770

THE GARBAGE MAN'S DAUGHTER Series by Gloria
Shell Mitchell is a work of creative nonfiction. The names
have been changed to protect the identities of the innocent,
or otherwise.

Scripture quotations are taken from the *Holy Bible,* New
Living Translation, copyright © 1996. Used by permission
of Tyndale House Publishers, Inc., Wheaton, Illinois 60189.
All rights reserved.

Presented by: EncourageMint Books
Gardena, CA 90249
www.encouragemintbooks.com
gloriashellmitchell@gmail.com

Cover Designer: mnsartstudio
Page Layout by: nosyrosydesigns@gmail.com
Editor: joy@joycmitchell.com
Proofreader: Addie Burroughs

Printed in the United States

DEDICATION

To children of divorce,
parents and school teachers.

SPECIAL THANKS

Martha Tucker, Coach and Developmental Editor

Dr. Joy Wassel, Critic and Confidante

Rev. Dorcas McReynolds, Reviewer

Pastor Luida Johnson, Reviewer

Rev. B. J. Jenkins, Encourager

Effie P. Javis, Encourager

Laura Shinn, Encourager

Rev. Sha' Givens, Coach

Fran Lewis, Reviewer

The Holy Spirit, Inspiration

My memoir critique group of
The Greater Los Angeles Writers Society

Joyce Actor, Group Leader

CONTENTS

AUTHOR'S NOTE

DAVIDA KINCAID, the eighth of eighteen children born to Blossom Cox Kincaid, experienced a dramatic and traumatic shift in comfort and responsibilities after her daddy, a garbage man employed by the city of Columbia, South Carolina, deserted his family. Her strong faith in God keeps her praying and believing that her parents will get back together one day and the family's living conditions will improve.

The aftermath of the family breakup is described in book one of the series, *The Garbage Man's Daughter: Letting Go of Shame.* Book two, *Letting Go of SECRETS* describes life with Daddy and Mama and the circumstances leading to separation. In book three, *Letting Go of STRESS,* Davida attempts to escape life in the country during her junior high years, and in the process, learns a lot about relationships. Book four, *Letting Go of SCARS,* describes her high school challenges and concerns during the civil rights era. Her nostalgic journey through the turbulent 60s notes people, places, products, practices, and phrases. Questions for self-reflection appear in the back of each book.

Based on a true story told from a child's perspective, Davida brings awareness to multiple issues that impact youths from impoverished and fractured families. She describes the power of a teacher to either inspire or destroy a child's will to achieve. When family support is lacking, she shares the pain of holding on to and the peace that results from letting go of garbage—negatives that influence thoughts, feelings, and behaviors. Davida speaks on behalf of children who had no voice in grown up business in the 1960s. Since young people remain innocent victims of divorce, separation, child support and custody battles, her message is applicable for today: Consider the children!

Chapter 1

LONGING FOR CHANGE

DADDY GOT AWAY SCOT-FREE, I thought, while standing at the kitchen stove stirring a pot of pinto beans on a gloomy afternoon in August 1962. The least he could do was buy food for us. Is a child better off living in a family that has been ripped apart like mine, or, living in fear that one parent will kill the other like my married sister's children?

Hearing Sam Cooke on the radio singing "A Change Is Gonna Come" reminded me of the big fight my nephews and I witnessed between Lynette, and her husband, Roscoe. Having one parent might be better than having two that don't get along.

I shuddered at the thought of the change that had come and gone in my life—my big escape from country living to life in New York City. During summer vacation I was happy in Brooklyn until Roscoe swung a lead pipe at Lynette's head. He looked like he wanted to hit a homerun. I was so scared that I *begged* to come back to the boondocks of Columbia, South Carolina.

Thoughts of what could have happened generated fresh tears. That fight made me wonder if I should stop hoping my mama and daddy would get back together even though they haven't seen or talked to each other in five years.

In the background I heard, "Oh there have been times that I thought I couldn't last for long, but now I think I'm able to carry on, It's been a long, long time coming, but I know a change gonna come, Oh, yes it will."

"I could have written that song," I murmured, adding salt to the beans in Mama's beat up aluminum double boiler and then turning the heat down to "simmer." My change from country to city living had come and gone. I'd have to wait for another opportunity like that. Meanwhile, I was glad we had already switched over from a wood stove to an electric one.

Listening to crying babies was a whole lot easier on my heart, eyes and ears than hearing Lynette scream. I learned to be careful what I ask for because I just might get it. I asked to leave home and I did. But I asked to come back, too. Only God stopped Roscoe from killing Lynette in front of his children and me. I wanted so much to stay in the city, but I couldn't risk having to be the one to tell Mama her daughter had been murdered.

I placed the lid on the pot and then went into the living room wondering if Roscoe had given me his old Ford after driving me back home so I wouldn't tell Mama he was beating up her daughter. I'd never know the truth about the car but I was certain he would regret ever laying hands on one of Blossom Kincaid's daughters if my eighteen-year-old sister Beverly ever jumped into a fight between him and Lynette.

I pictured Beverly telling Roscoe, "You ran Davida back home, but you don't scare me!"

An idea came to mind. Just because I was the oldest and tallest child at home didn't mean I had to work the hardest. Everybody should help out around the house now that Mama had found a job.

I ran out on the front porch and yelled to the children playing in the yard.

"Come in the living room right now!"

Then I went inside and turned down the radio volume while I stood and waited.

First came my five stair-step little sisters, ten-year-old Vera carrying our one-year-old baby brother Andrew, followed by eight-year-old April, six-year-old Gladys, four-year-old Barbara Jean, and two-year-old Carrie. My twelve-year-old brother Harry, who never liked to listen to me, took baby steps as he walked beside Sylvester, our four-year-old nephew whose mother, Zenobia, had died when he was two. Vera sat Andrew down on the floor at her feet.

I counted nine people including myself, and then said, "Since I'm fourteen and the oldest child at home, I need everybody to do what I say. Mama can't afford to take one day off work because she makes more in tips than the Jackson Hotel pays her for cleaning rooms all day. Understand?"

"Yeah! Uh huh! Okay," they said. Looking around I saw heads nodding.

Andrew nodded his head, too. Everybody laughed, except me. They knew he didn't understand, and I did too, but I was trying to be a tough big sister. I was serious about what I said and I didn't think they would obey me if they thought I was softhearted.

"I like washing dishes," Vera said. "April can help me."

"I'll dry them," eight-year-old April said. "I hate washing dishes."

"I'll sweep the yard, clip the hedges and make sure we have wood for the fireplace," Harry said. "Sylvester can help me work outdoors so we boys don't have to be around you girls."

"I knew it was too good to believe you would cooperate without saying something smart," I said. "You can wipe that smirk off your face–"

"What can I do?" six-year-old Gladys asked.

"You can dust the furniture, and I'll show you how," I said. She grinned like she was proud to have an important job.

"Barbara Jean, you're a big four-year-old. You can help Vera bring in clothes off the clothesline and she'll show you how to fold diapers. Okay?"

"K," she said.

Carrie and Andrew, just pick up behind yourselves so nobody trips over toys you leave on the floor. All right?"

Carrie nodded her head like it was a yo-yo on a string. She looked so cute. I couldn't hold back my smile even though I tried to look stern.

"Andrew, raise your hand high," I said, lifting up my hand like I was in court swearing in. He raised his hand and everybody smiled.

I didn't understand why one-year-old Andrew was slow walking, slow talking, slow eating and way too slow understanding potty training. But he had been quick to pee in my face the first time I changed his diaper.

Mama told us the doctor said my baby brother was born retarded. I didn't know what retarded meant exactly, but I knew it wasn't his fault he couldn't think fast. I tried to include Andrew in everything we did so he wouldn't feel left out. God must have intended for people without birth defects to look after people who have them. Andrew helped me realize how my life could have been very different.

"Listen," I said. "Every school year I try not to miss a day so I can earn a perfect attendance certificate. I want to learn everything my teachers know so I'll be smart. Mama doesn't know it yet, but when I grow up I'm going to go to college so I can get a good job and make enough money to buy her a big house in the city."

"When you gonna do that?" Barbara Jean said.

"Say, when *are* you *going to* do that?" I said. "When I grow up. It's going to be a surprise. Don't tell Mama what I said. Now zip your lips."

I put my index finger and thumb together and yanked my hand across my lips.

"It's your turn," I said.

They zipped their lips, too, including stubborn Harry, to my surprise. Andrew watched, raised his arm and then made a s-l-o-w backward zip. We watched and waited for him to finish and then clapped. It tickled me to see him smile.

"Okay. My secret is safe," I said. "It's my job to cook dinner everyday. And now, let's eat."

"Yea!" Sylvester said. "Food!"

"Boy, eating should be your middle name!" I said. "I don't understand why you still look like a weasel. Where does your food go?"

He laughed as they all hurried into the kitchen ahead of me and took their place at the table. April and Gladys stood while Barbara Jean and Sylvester sat down, two to a chair. Carrie climbed on a wood chair and stood up. Nobody wanted to share her seat because she was a messy eater. Vera put Andrew in the highchair and the rest of us stood because we didn't have enough chairs for everybody to sit.

I fixed nine plates of beans and rice starting from the youngest to the oldest child, adding a little more to match each growing body. I was careful to make sure that everybody had a fair share and Mama's dinner was left in the oven. Nobody touched the food until I finished serving everyone.

Harry said Daddy's favorite blessing, "Grace in the kitchen, grace in the hall. Please for God's sake, don't eat it all. Amen." We laughed like we always did when he said that grace.

Beneath the sounds of smacking lips and spoons scraping Melmac plates, I heard the song *Big Girls Don't Cry* by The Four Seasons. The people singing that song must not have problems like I do, I thought, wishing we had more food so everybody could have enough to eat. My meal of beans, rice and cornbread soon disappeared off everyone's plate. I watched Sylvester lap bean broth like he was a puppy. Harry sopped his broth with a hunk of cornbread and took big bites. Barbara Jean held her empty plate to her face and licked it, while Andrew picked up one bean at a time and nibbled on it. Somebody would be glad to get his leftovers. I felt like crying at our "po" meal, but I didn't.

My family was rich in love and we were all together.

Well, most of us. Then I remembered my missing sisters and smiled to hold back tears. I loved all of them, including Beverly, who just didn't know how to receive my love. Our home was a lot more peaceful with her not there to complain about my cooking.

Filling Zenobia's role as the oldest child at home made me sad and scared at the same time. She had become the oldest when Mama's firstborn son died of pneumonia at thirteen. Then she died at twenty-one after a miscarriage caused her to bleed to death. I missed my big sister. She told us never to say bad words and I didn't, except the one time I said *butt*. I didn't even know it was a bad word. That one whupping flattened my bottom into a pancake and taught me to say fanny, booty, rump, behind... anything but butt. I hoped I'd never have to whup my little brothers and sisters.

I stared at Sylvester, Zenobia's son, thinking, he'll never know his mama and his daddy is somewhere out there, just like ours. Dang! Did God make men stronger than women just so they could make babies and run away?

Chapter 2
HUNGER IN THE LAND OF PLENTY

FRIDAY NIGHT I WENT TO BED EXPECTING to sleep late the next day. With Mama working, I thought I wouldn't have to take the three-mile hike to the bus stop anymore to go get food money from Daddy. But I was wrong.

Mama woke me up early Saturday morning like she always did.

"Davida, I need you to go get money from David," she said.

"No Mama, I don't want to go meet Daddy," I groaned. I pulled the covers over my head and curled up in a tight ball on the rollaway in the middle of the living room floor. I didn't know which I hated most, her waking me early or having to take that long walk. "What about the tips you get?"

"Tips? What about 'em?" she said, standing right over me. "They just a help. I make three dollars a day but I won't get paid 'til next week 'cause they hold back a week's pay. Besides, David know ya'll still gotta eat and git shoes on your feet while money burn a hole in his pocket. We ain't never had plenty, even when he brought his pay home. These children might starve next week if you don't go."

"Awww Mama!" I rolled over, stretched my arms and legs, and pushed back the covers. She was leaning over me wearing her pink housecoat and a pink rag tied around her head. Why did I have to go to work and she didn't?

Knowing she had succeeded in waking me up, she went back into her bedroom.

Mama knew I wouldn't go back to sleep.

"Being the oldest is no fun," I said, dragging myself out of bed. I smoothed out the wrinkled sheets and folded the rollaway before pushing it into Mama's room. I washed up in the hand basin, dressed in a hurry, and then ran out the door wishing I had some cornflakes or a honey bun.

I hurried down Cashmere Road with a quarter in my hand to catch the nine o'clock bus. The next one wouldn't come until one o'clock in the afternoon, too late for me to be standing outside the gate of the City Shed at noon when he knocked off work.

My quarter spun around and settled on top of other coins in the glass fare box as I waited for the white bus driver to punch a hole in my transfer. I wondered if he earned more sitting all day than men who lifted heavy garbage cans. The bus jerked and made me lunge past all the empty seats in the front as I scurried toward the rear seats for colored people.

The bus passed a house where thick black smoke was rising amongst the trees in the backyard. As we got closer, I saw a tall lady poking a blazing fire in a ditch beside the house. She was burning garbage. Daddy was fortunate to get paid for his city job. Country folks didn't need his help.

I thought about the first Saturday that I had gone to meet my daddy on payday. After a parade of garbage trucks rolled into the City Shed parking lot, Daddy, like most of the garbagemen, strutted off the yard like a peacock with a thousand dollars in his pocket. I was surprised to see nothing but one-dollar bills wrapped in a twenty when he unrolled his dough.

"That sure is a lot of ones for all your hard work!" I said, thinking I was pumping him up with praise. I remembered that Drunk Mr. Fred, Mama's used-to-be boyfriend, gave her twenty dollars every Friday before he wasted the rest of his pay on liquor.

"Low pay beat no pay," he growled.

"Yessir," I hushed. Mind your own business, Davida, I thought.

Daddy counted and then handed me five one-dollar bills.

I was grateful.

On his payday I wasn't the only one ready to meet him. The people in his three favorite liquor apartments in Nixon Homes probably turned to the page with his name on it and started keeping a tab before he even showed up. Everybody knew he was famous for saying, "I drink gin 'cause it ain't no sin." He proved it with a big liquor bill that he had to pay on every Saturday before he could buy more.

I felt like Daddy and his drinking buddies were robbed blind by having to pay a dollar for a shot of liquor. They emptied that glass with one gulp.

"Drunk people do some crazy things," I mumbled. I looked around to see if anybody on the bus had heard me. Nobody seemed to notice. I didn't want them to think I was crazy because I was sitting there talking to myself.

I closed my eyes and rested my head against the window. When I woke up the bus had stopped in front of Belk's Department Store on Main Street. I saw a colored lady boarding with two shopping bags as I rushed out the backdoor. If Daddy stopped spending more money on liquor than on food, then I could be like that lady and buy something instead of wasting time window-shopping.

A few hours later I spotted Daddy coming toward the City Shed exit gate. He was walking and talking with another man on the other side of the chain-linked fence. I waved at them, thinking, I can't believe he's still smoking after all that coughing he used to do before he got sick with TB.

Both of them held a cigarette. They stopped for a moment while Daddy reached over with his lighter and lit the other man's cigarette. When they approached the gate, I recognized Mr. Joe, Daddy's work partner for many

years. He looked cool as he tilted his head back and blew
smoke rings in the air with his mouth. Smoke came out of
Daddy's nose like it was a chimney.

Daddy smiled and walked toward me. "There my
daughter. When I see Davida, I know she want money."

"Yes, Sir. You know Mama sends me to get food
money," I said.

He pulled a dollar bill out of his pocket and handed it
to me. "That's all I can spare today."

I stared at the bill in my hand. Was he joking?

He saw the hurt look on my face, but he didn't say
anything about it.

"I need bus fare back home," I said. "What can I get
with a dollar?"

He patted his pocket, then turned and yelled, "Joe, got
a quarter I can have?" The man reached in his pocket and
tossed Daddy a quarter. He caught it and handed it to me.

"Thank you," I said, hoping he'd hear disappointment
in my voice. If he did, he didn't say anything about it.

"Tell yo mama I'll do better next week," he said.

He and Mr. Joe left me standing at the gate. They
walked away puffing their cigarettes and leaving a trail
of smoke behind.

"Which house you wanna hit first?" Mr. Joe said as
they headed toward Nixon Homes.

Daddy was smoking like he'd forgotten all about the
coughing spells he used to have before he got sick with
TB. Mama used to hide his cigarettes, but he hasn't had to
worry about her ever since we moved to Cashmere Road
out in the country.

I tucked the bill in my windbreaker pocket and headed
for the bus stop, thinking, Mama's going to need a lot of
tips next week. She'd have to decide how to spend the
dollar because I didn't know what to buy.

Downtown I window-shopped until time to catch the
last bus to the country at five o'clock. I dreamed of the
day when I could go inside the stores and buy whatever
I wanted. I remembered my shopping spree the day after

Christmas when I was in fifth grade. Mama's cousins Lula Belle and Lucille had given me twenty dollars for my birthday, and I caught a big sale on black and white saddle oxfords and roller skates. Walking out of that store with everything I wanted and money still in my pocket made me feel rich and powerful. How I wished I could do that again.

On the bus ride home I kept wondering what Mama was going to say about the dollar bill. When I walked in the house she was sitting on the sofa hemming a pair of Harry's pants.

"Here's your food money," I said, handing her the dollar. I felt sorry that I let her down by not bringing home more, but she knew Daddy better than I did.

She didn't seem a bit surprised.

I plopped down beside her, tired after the long walk from the bus stop.

Mama dropped the pants in her lap and stared at the dollar.

"Oh. Daddy said he'll have more money next week," I said.

She glanced at me and shook her head.

"David can act ugly when he want to," she said. "I'll never forget the time he told Zenobia to come meet him on payday and he'd give her some money. Zenobia was so excited she paid two dollars for a taxi ride to the City Shed. Shold 'nough, her daddy gave her some money —a one dollar bill. She caught the bus back home for a quarter." Mama chuckled. "That thang hurt Zenobia so bad that she cried and cried. She swore David would never trick her like that again."

Mama laughed at her own story.

"He's not going to trick me like that if I can help it," I said. "Next time, I'll keep on begging until he pays me to leave him alone. I'm sorry I failed you, Mama."

"Ain't yo fault," she said. "Good luck. We gonna have to trust God to get us through next week. Maybe somebody'll give me a real big tip."

I went into the bathroom and stared at the girl in the mirror. Suddenly, I got the urge to practice begging. I made pitiful faces and said please, trying to see how many different ways I could say the word until I sounded like a convincing beggar. I wouldn't mind being a nuisance if I got a favorable response.

I walked out of the bathroom thinking, "Next Saturday, I'll be ready for Daddy."

***

School lunches and Mrs. Johnson helped to feed us all week long. On Friday after school I started to cook dinner but didn't find one bag of black-eyed peas or dried beans when I opened the shiny silver ten-gallon grocery can on the floor. I stared at the partial bags of flour, rice, sugar, meal and grits, and then closed the lid to keep the roaches out.

What could I cook? I opened the refrigerator and pulled out some fatback, our daily meat. It was cheap and plentiful and served the dual-purpose of making grease to season beans and to fry other foods. I sliced and fried the fatback, wondering what to fix with it to make a meal.

Popping grease is dangerous. After turning each slice in the cast iron skillet, I ran across the room and waited until the hot grease stopped popping. Getting burned once was enough to teach me to escape. Everybody at school recognized a grease burn on somebody's face and arms, and a straightening comb burn on the nape of the neck. Burns spoke louder than words and nobody was going to poke fun at me if I could help it.

"Well God, I need a miracle," I said, looking up at the ceiling. "Long ago my Sunday School teacher told me to pray about everything because you promised to supply all our needs. So I'm telling you I need to feed all these hungry people and one small slice of bacon is not enough."

Thinking God might drop food on the table, I made a pitcher of cherry Kool-Aid. While putting it in the refrigerator to chill, I noticed a ten-pound sack of Irish potatoes in the vegetable bin and a great idea came to me. These will work.

I grabbed a butcher knife and started peeling potatoes and singing, "My mother and father were Irish, my mother and father were Irish, my mother and father were Irish, so I am Irish too. We bought a sack of potatoes, we bought a sack of potatoes, we bought a sack of potatoes, for they are Irish too...."

Vera peeped through the opening in the café curtains that separated the kitchen from the living room. She saw the huge pile of potato slices I'd put in a ceramic bowl half full of water so they wouldn't turn brown.

"What are we going to make with all those potatoes?" she said.

"French fries," I said, dropping a handful in the skillet.

She watched as I ran away from the splashing grease when the water hit it.

"Ouch!" I cried. I hadn't moved fast enough. A drop of the hot liquid splashed out and landed on my wrist. "Ahhh Vera!" I ran to the refrigerator and grabbed a stick of oleomargarine and rubbed it on my wrist. It melted into my skin and soothed the sting.

I was glad Mama had taught me to spread butter or ice on a burn right away to prevent blistering. I resented being distracted, but I didn't get angry. Vera didn't understand that cooking was serious business.

"Can I help?" she said, staring at my buttered wrist.

"Today we're going to have a French fry eating contest," I said. "Go tell everybody to come to the table. They'll be excited to hear me say, 'Eat as much as you want'."

Vera ran through the living room hollering, "Come and get it!" The front screen door slammed shut as she ran outside yelling, "Extra, extra, come play a dinner game!"

She made me more excited about my idea. While Vera rounded up everybody, I stacked a mountain of French fries on a sheet of wax paper in the center of the table.

Everybody, except Harry, came running into the kitchen. Vera pointed to the hand basin on a little wicker table that Grandpa Cox had found in his boss' garbage.

"Line up and wash your hands before you take your place at the table," she said.

I was thrilled to see my next oldest sister growing up to be the second in command at home. She was making it easier for me to leave when the right time came.

"Vera, thanks for helping me," I said, as I set a Melmac plate in front of each person. "First we'll bless our food and then I'll tell you the special thing we're going to do today. Bow your head and close your eyes so we can say grace together."

I prayed. "God is great, God is good, God we thank you for this food. By your hand must all be fed. Give us Lord our daily bread. Amen."

They opened their eyes and stared at me.

"We're going to have a French fry eating contest," I announced.

The smiles on their faces let me know they were excited about having a different kind of dinner.

"Everybody will get five fries to start. When you finish eating those five, then you can take one fry at a time from the stack in the middle of the table. After you eat it you must count aloud saying six, then seven, then eight.... Today you may eat all you want. You may stop whenever you get enough. The person who eats the most fries will be the winner."

"What do we get if we win?" April said.

"Oh, you get to be called the champion or winner," slid off my tongue.

"Champion. I like that," she said.

"Now wait until I say, 'Go!'" I walked around dropping five fries on each plate with a pair of long-handled tongs. Vera followed behind me, placing a slice of bacon and squeezing Heinz Ketchup on the rim of the worn-out plates. After the food had been served I noticed that everyone except the youngest two had both hands hovering over their plates.

"Everybody except Carrie and Andrew put your hands down by your side," I said. "They can put their hands on the table because their arms are shorter."

"No, that's not fair!" Barbara Jean said.

"I'm still gonna win!" Sylvester said.

"No, I'm gonna win," April said. "I couldn't say that if Harry was here."

I had fun waiting for them to quiet down. They made sure nobody cheated.

"Ready! Get Set! Go!" I shouted, waving my right hand.

I laughed as they dipped French fries in catsup and pushed fries in their mouths like logs going through a sawmill. Carrie tried to chew too fast and gagged a couple of times. Each one had a glass of Kool-Aid to wash the fries down. They looked around at each other but nobody said a word. Besides my laughter, all I heard was smacking and gulp, gulp.

The stack of fries in the middle of the table was dwindling fast when Gladys said, "I give up. I'm full!"

"Me too," Carrie said after eating only five fries.

"I'll eat your share!" Sylvester said, with his jaw poking out.

One by one they dropped out of the race. Finally April said, "All right Sylvester, you win! I'll burst wide open if I eat one more fry. Fifteen is all I can eat."

"Well, there's only two left," he said. "When I eat them that will make twenty-two for me. I win!"

I walked over and lifted his right arm. "Ladies and gentlemen, today's champion of the French fry eating contest is none other than Sylvester!"

Everybody clapped as Sylvester raised his arm while still chewing.

"I told ya'll I was gonna win before we started," he bragged.

"We already knew you were going to win," Vera said. "You never get enough to eat."

I laughed. Vera was right. Sylvester, the clean up boy, always ate our leftovers. That contest made me realize that I was a much happier person when I learned to use what we had in a fun way, rather than complain about what we didn't have, what used to be, or things we couldn't change. My attitude got an adjustment.

Mama came in after we finished the contest. I handed her the pan containing a slice of bacon and seven warm French fries that I had hidden in the oven for her.

"This shold is a po dinner," she said, while headed toward the living room carrying her plate. Then she plopped down on the sofa.

The little ones crowded around her, saying, "Mama, dinner was fun today! I'm so full! You missed it! I want to do that again!"

"I ate all my food today," little Carrie said, tugging Mama's skirt tail.

It didn't take much to make them happy. They had no idea that potatoes were all we had. I felt like crying, but would I shed tears of sadness or tears of joy?

Harry walked in and they told him all about the dinner game.

"Shucks, I missed the French fry contest, Sis," he said. "Tell me when you're going to do it again."

"If you only knew the truth," I giggled, proud that I had managed to camouflage our lack of food choices. I wanted to pat myself on the back because Mama had said we might starve this week. But we didn't. We'd had stewed potatoes and rice before, but this was the first time that potatoes were the whole meal.

After everyone had left the kitchen, I sat down at the table and ate the few fries I'd saved for myself. Maybe I was skinny because I didn't mind skipping a meal if it meant that the little ones could have a full tummy. I nibbled to make the meal last longer.

Before going to bed, I went to the bathroom to practice begging one last time before going to meet Daddy on Saturday. Staring at my face in the mirror, I said, "please, please, please" like James Brown. Begging is not for everybody, but I was desperate enough to do it.

"Tomorrow, I'll be ready for Daddy," I said. "I'll act like a buzzing fly until he pays me to get out of his face."

Chapter 3

IT COSTS TOO MUCH

I STOOD AT THE GATE TO THE CITY SHED watching Daddy and his work partner walk toward me. Mr. Joe nodded and kept going when Daddy stopped and pulled a five-dollar bill from the cash rolled up in his hand.

"We almost starved last week," I cried.

Daddy's hand froze. I looked up at him, frowned, batted my eyes and said, "Last night we had nothing but French fries for dinner."

He stared at me and then pushed back the five and pulled out a ten. "All righty then. Take this," he said, handing me the bill. "I'm in a hurry. Joe and me got sumin special to do today. Tell yo mama I give you all I can spare."

"Yessir! Thank you so much!" Now that's more like it, I thought. I grinned, threw my arms around him, stood on my tippy toes and kissed his prickly cheek. He needed a shave.

Daddy smiled and stuck out his chest. Then he rushed off to catch up with Mr. Joe. I think he was proud of himself for making me so happy.

Practicing begging had paid off. I skipped away singing, "I got it, I got it, I got it!" The victory made my body tingle. I'd have to do that again.

I went to the A&P grocery store near the bus stop and pushed a metal shopping basket through the aisles, looking for items Mama had scribbled on a list. Even though *suger, flar, fatbak,* and other words weren't spelled correctly, I had no trouble figuring them out because I had plenty of practice reading her writing.

Without paying attention to prices, I dropped into my basket all the staples—dried beans, rice, grits, self-rising flour, cornmeal and sugar. Mama said those "rough groceries" would stretch far enough to feed a family.

Standing at the check out counter, I watched the glass window on the cash register as the cashier punched in the cost of each item until a total sale of $13.43 popped up. Shocked, I stared at the cashier, thinking about my ten dollars. I'd forgotten all about sales tax.

She read my face. "Do you need to put some things back?" she said.

"Yes."

"How much money do you have?"

"Ten dollars," I said. I felt embarrassed because other people were standing in line behind me.

"You can put back the five-pound bags of sugar and flour and get two-pound bags instead," she suggested. "Then I'll ring up that total."

I took the two items off the conveyor belt, left my cart at the register and ran to the dry goods aisle to exchange them. When I returned, the cashier rang up the new total and the register showed $10.69.

Gosh! Still too high, I thought.

"You've got two packs of wieners that cost 99 cents each," she said. "I'll take off one pack and that should do it." She put a pack of wieners on one side of the register and got a new total of $9.75.

"Perfect," I said.

It didn't bother the cashier to make people wait while she helped me, but I felt angry eyes piercing my back for holding up the line. After giving me my quarter change, she doubled a big brown paper sack and filled it with groceries while I watched. I wondered how to estimate the total cost and include the sales tax next time. When she finished, I thanked her, and then wrapped my arms around the sack and headed for the bus stop.

After boarding the bus, I plopped down and put the groceries in my lap. I was happy not to have the five pound bags of flour and sugar, and even happier that I remembered to keep a quarter for bus fare. I hate having to always think like a grown up. Life was so much simpler when I was a little girl.

I fell asleep until the bus turned on Cashmere Road where I got off. I shifted the heavy bag from one arm to the other as I walked the three miles home. Although I asked God to let somebody stop and give me a ride all or even part of the way home, He didn't answer my prayer. Experience had taught me to keep on walking instead of standing at the bus stop, wishing and waiting.

Vera ran outside and grabbed the bag when I turned into the path leading to our front door. She rescued me moments before I dropped from exhaustion.

"Oh, Vera! My tired arms say thank you," I said. "Every little bit of help around here feels good to me. Mama was right when she said, 'Something is better than nothing.'" I rested both hands on my hips and followed her inside.

"You looked like you couldn't take another step," Vera said. "And Mama also says, 'Many hands make light work.' Maybe that's why she's got so many children."

"Yeah. Maybe. She's got a saying for everything."

That Saturday was the first of several embarrassing ten-dollar shopping sprees that forced me to learn how to estimate by rounding each item to one dollar as I dropped it in the basket. Some people were nice enough to offer me a few cents if that's all I needed, but it hurt my pride to ask anybody for money, except Daddy.

One day I had to put several items back and I got annoyed with the young cashier and told her, "Sales tax ought to be included in every posted price so people will know right away if they have enough money to buy something they want!"

"I just work here," she said.

I felt bad for getting upset with her.

Grocery shopping was a good math lesson. Not only did I learn how to add quickly and accurately in my head, I also learned how to recognize bargains. Sometimes I ended up with change left over. Every week I shopped and carried home ten dollars or more worth of food.

Then one Saturday I showed up and found the City Shed gate locked and nobody on the yard. I knew Daddy's address but I'd never been to his room. I walked across town to the Five Points area and knocked on the front door. A lady answered and told me Daddy's entrance was in the rear of her house. I went back there and knocked on room number 3, but he didn't answer.

I remembered that Mrs. Moss, my fourth grade teacher, said her house was directly across the street from Daddy's. I went to visit her, hoping she'd give me bus fare if I couldn't find him. She was the first person I'd told that my mama and daddy had separated. That little old lady with a bun in her hair was nice enough to listen. She hugged me when I cried and invited me to stop by her house whenever I visited him.

Please let her be at home, I thought as I walked along the concrete sidewalk lined with ivy. The brass handle on her wooden front door clanged as I knocked three times, hoping Daddy would come home while I waited at her house.

I wondered if Mrs. Moss would remember me from five years ago until she pulled back the white curtain covering the glass and smiled at me. The lock clicked.

"Hello Davida," she said, swinging open the door. "It's been a long time." She stepped aside and made a hand gesture for me to come inside. She seemed as glad to see me as I was to see her.

"Hey Mrs. Moss," I said. "I'm going to my daddy's house across the street, but I remembered that you said you lived right in front of him. Thank you again for helping me when he first left us."

"How nice to see you again," she said. "I'm just cleaning up after a luncheon for ladies I call my sorority sisters. Since you're here, why don't you come in and have some of the leftovers. Maybe you can take some to your daddy. It's just too much food to throw away and I can't eat it all by myself. Will you do me that favor?"

"Well, I do have about thirty minutes," I said.

"Excellent! You've only grown taller. Otherwise, you look the same." She hugged me as I passed by her. The hug reassured me that she would give me bus fare if I needed it.

Too bad she never had children of her own, I thought. She would have been a great mother.

Mrs. Moss pointed to a seat at a long table with fancy glass dishes loaded with all kinds of food. My eyes darted from dish to dish like a fly nibbling on everybody's plate at a picnic. Cakes and pies covered one end of the table. I was sure I knew how Hansel and Gretel felt when they found the gingerbread house. I wanted to taste everything but I didn't want to act hungry or be greedy.

"Help yourself," Mrs. Moss said, handing me a white plate with the word china stamped on it. Could she tell that I hadn't eaten breakfast?

She limped into the kitchen while I filled a plate with fried catfish, collard greens, salad, ambrosia, succotash, baked chicken, candied yams, tomato wedges, yeast rolls, banana pudding, and moist pineapple upside down cake. I gobbled it up and washed it all down with sweet tea while Mrs. Moss was busy banging pots and pans.

Looking at my empty plate, I felt guilty eating all that food while the children in my house were hungry, especially Sylvester. I wondered why some people have so much while others are starving. It just didn't seem fair.

"The meal was delicious," I said, getting up from the table. "Thank you so much for my full tummy." I rubbed my belly and smiled.

An empty plate tells the cook the food was good, Mama liked to say.

Mrs. Moss came out of the kitchen as fast as a person with two good legs could walk, bringing an aluminum pan that she began filling with food. "I'm glad you enjoyed it. Take with you as much as you want," she said.

I wished I could take enough food for my whole family, but quickly squashed that thought. How would I get it home?

She handed me the heavy container stuffed with food and covered with Reynolds Wrap. "Take this to your daddy," she said. "Tell him he can keep the pan."

"I hate to eat and run but I don't want to miss my daddy."

"Come back again when you have more time to talk," she said. "Here's a quarter for bus fare when you do."

"Oh, I will," I said, "Thank you for everything." I hugged her and then ran across the street clutching the pan of goodies. How did she know I needed bus fare? Amazing!

"God, you led me to a free feast when I couldn't even buy a hot dog." I said. "Thank you for giving me this day my daily bread, plus meat, plus dessert, plus sweet tea and more!"

I went back to Daddy's room and knocked. No answer. I sat down on the concrete steps leading down to his rented room beneath the woman's house and waited. The pan of food was in my lap to avoid attracting ants. "God please send Daddy home so I can get back downtown in time to catch the last bus to the country," I prayed.

I spent a lot of time talking silently to God and crying while waiting. "You know I hate my life in the country. I've already tried living other places but I hated them, too. I want to know if any married couples are happy with each other. Do other children's daddy send money home for them? Why am I the only child out here begging for money from her father? I don't understand why my family has to be so different." I shook my head.

While I was complaining to God, Daddy showed up. He came along whistling his favorite song by Ray Charles, "I've got a woman, way cross town, and she's good to me." I jumped up off the steps and yelled, "There you are!" I marveled at the way God heard and answered my prayer.

"We knocked off early today 'cause of a funeral'," Daddy said, going down the steps that led to his room. The ceiling was very low. He leaned his head forward and went through the narrow entrance under the house. I leaned over and followed him. The house was level but the ground beneath it was slanted. Inside I saw storage boxes stacked from the floor to the ceiling. We couldn't stand erect until after we reached the community bathroom at the end of a hallway. Daddy's room was on the left side next to the bathroom. Across the hall were two other rented rooms.

After opening the lock that hung outside the door, he went inside and slung his hat on a nail in the wall. Then he fell across the double bed that took up most of the space in the tiny room while I pushed aside things on a cluttered wooden table to clear a spot for the big pan of food that would not fit in his little icebox.

The odor of mildew was strong. I pulled open the window to let some fresh air come inside and a dim light flooded the room. I looked up and saw the woman's paved driveway outside.

"How can you stand the smell in here?" I said.

"I don't smell nuttin," he said. "I guess I'm used to it."

I went to the bathroom and found a bottle of Lysol that had never been opened. After running hot water on the cap to unscrew it, I wiped the disinfectant on the walls, floors, table, and windowsill in Daddy's room. The two odors mingled and made me want to puke. I needed to leave, pronto.

My daddy seemed to live outdoors like a dog, but not exactly. How could he appreciate living like that when he used to move around inside our whole house? He'd told me the rooms used to be slave quarters beneath the master's house.

I frowned at the thought of humans living like animals. At least we don't have to live underground. My daddy and two other men lived beneath the elderly Negro woman's house. Daddy's ceiling squeaked every time she walked in her kitchen. I couldn't understand how Negroes could let their own people live like that. Was this what people called "city living?" If so, I'd rather stay in the country.

"I brought you some food. Do you want something to eat?"

Daddy snorted and began a drunken lecture. "Your mama cheated on me." His funky breath contaminated the foul air.

I tuned him out. I didn't want to hear that grownup talk. There was nothing I could do about it anyway. Standing in that tiny room with nothing but a bed and table for a hotplate and dirty icebox with crusty spilled milk stuck to the bottom, I wondered how the daddy I loved ended up in a place like that. He looked disgusting as I listened to his snores between talking nonsense.

Finding a paper plate, I fixed him some of the food but didn't give it to him. He'd eat when he sobered up a bit.

I had a flashback of the despicable Drunk Mr. Fred, Mama's old boyfriend. "God, why do people spend all that money on a drink that makes them feel bad?"

"Daddy, give me some money?" I said between snores. He didn't answer right away so I spoke a bit louder. "Daddy, I need some money now so I can go catch the bus." Still no answer. The third time I shook his mattress and yelled, "Daddy give me some money now so I can go!" He made two "snort, snort" sounds and I knew I had gotten his attention. Without saying a word, he rolled over, reached in his pocket, pulled out a five-dollar bill, and laid it on the bed. There was no bulge in his pocket so I figured that was all he had.

At least I got something, I thought, picking up the five. Knowing Daddy would rather drink liquor than eat, I grabbed the pan of food, said a quick goodbye and left. I ran to the end of the block praying the whole time, "Please don't let me miss my bus." At the corner I saw people boarding the bus on the opposite side of the street. Two people were waiting in line.

"Now all I need is for the light to change so the bus can't go. Surely you won't let me get this close and miss it," I said. The light turned red as the last person stepped on board. I dashed across the street and the bus driver reopened the door for me.

"Whew!" I sat down and patted the top of the heavy pan I'd placed in my lap. This will get us through the weekend, I thought. Mama will have to buy food next week. It was hard enough for me to get the money.

Chapter 4
An Unexpected Change

THE NEXT SATURDAY HAD A TERRIBLE start, but a terrific finish. My bus broke down and the gate to the City Shed was locked by the time I arrived that sunny November afternoon. After searching for Daddy in Nixon Homes, I walked across town to his room and knocked. No answer. Needing bus fare, I sat on the steps, cuddled under my sweater, waited, watched, and prayed that he would come home with money in time for me to catch the last bus home.

"Boo!" A man said.

"Uh!" I said, opening my eyes. I jumped up wondering where I was. Then I saw Daddy standing at the bottom of the steps, grinning. I hadn't seen him smile in years.

"Davida, didn't I tell you last week you don't hafta wait for me no mo?"

"What? No sir. You didn't tell me anything last week but how Mama cheated on you."

"Well, looka here. I set up dishere account for you at Hamilton's Grocery Store down on the corner. I fixed it so you can buy up to twenty dollars wortha food."

"For real! You didn't tell me anything about that!"

"They know you come ev'ry Sad'day. I just hafta remember to pay the bill."

"Thank you so much!" I tripped while running down the steps to hug him, but he caught me. He didn't stagger or slobber when I hugged him.

"I shold know you glad after all the years you been coming," he said.

"You're right. I'm so happy," I said, choked up. I started to leave then turned back and said, "Oh, I need a quarter."

He stuck out his palm and I grabbed my bus fare. He knew what I needed. We both laughed. On my way up the steps I hollered, "I've got to hurry so I won't miss the last bus to the country."

The back of my sweater probably looked like Superman's cape flapping in the wind as I flew to the corner store. Was I dreaming? Instead of begging for ten dollars, I got double without asking. Wow! Does Daddy feel sorry for me after all these years of meeting him every Saturday? Is he trying to keep me out of his sight forever? Hmmm... maybe he's got a girlfriend.

I stopped running and opened the top button on my sweater before I turned the corner. I pressed down my bangs so I could look calm to the people inside. They don't need to see how excited I am, I thought. I felt bashful, even a little scared to walk into a store where I'd never been before to tell strangers I wanted to shop with no money. The thought of buying twenty dollars worth of food without a list made me eager to see what I could get.

A pregnant Negro cashier spoke to me as soon as I walked in. She was the first cashier I'd ever seen seated, instead of standing, at the cash register.

"Hey. Umm, I want to purchase food on David Kincaid's account," I said. "I'm his daughter, Davida."

She flipped the pages in a big Ledger book next to the register then smiled and said, "Okay. You go right ahead. His limit is twenty dollars."

"Thank you," I giggled. Don't let anybody pinch me and tell me I'm dreaming, I thought. I pushed a shopping cart all over the store that wasn't as big as Piggly Wiggly or A&P, but big enough. All the shelves were piled high with foods. I got the staples first. Then I put a large box of corn flakes in my buggy. The cash register in my head kept ringing as I got thin-sliced bologna, American cheese slices, and other foods including cans of Spam, potted meat and Eatwell Sardines.

Mama's going to be shocked, I thought, pushing my cart to the register. The total with tax was $19.59.

That's close enough! I thought, congratulating my brain for doing a fine job.

As the cashier bagged the groceries she said, "We deliver. Where do you live?"

"Live? Oh, I live a long way from here," I said.

"And where is that?" she asked.

"I live way past Ridgewood on Cashmere Road." I wanted her to stop asking me questions so I could hurry to the bus stop.

"Then how are you going to take all this food home?" she said.

I hadn't noticed that everything didn't fit in one big brown bag. I hadn't even thought about not being able to carry the double blessing in my arms. Even though the bus stop was across the street from the store, I still had to walk three miles when I got off on Cashmere Road.

"I don't know," I said, staring at the two bags. "I never bought this much food before." How was I going to get the food home?

"Wait here a minute," she said. She left and went to the back of the store to talk to a Negro man inside an office behind a glass window. I paced the floor around the register wondering what to do. The bus would soon be there. I needed her to hurry.

"The lady returned, wobbling like she would drop her big stomach at any minute. "I talked to my daddy. He lives in Ridgewood. He said if you can wait until the store closes, then we'll take you home with the groceries. Do you want to do that?"

"Really? I mean, sure," I said. "Thanks a lot. I'll wait."

I felt a big grin spread all across my face. Her news sounded too good to be true. I felt like shouting hallelujah.

"We're a Christian family and we're glad to help," she said, smiling. "You're welcome to wait here. Please put your bags beneath the counter for me until it's time to go." She placed both hands on her hips and leaned back like she was stretching while I put my bags out of sight.

"What's your name?" I asked.

"Oh, I'm Amanda. My daddy owns this store. Do you like to read?" she said on her way back behind the counter.

"Yes," I said, thinking, It's nice that she can see her daddy every day.

"You're welcome to read any of the magazines on the rack while you wait," she said. "Ebony and Jet are the most popular." She glanced at her watch. "It's almost four o'clock. We close at seven."

"Thank you, again," I said. The words didn't seem adequate for all she'd done to help me. I went back to the magazine rack and read the November 1962 issue of Ebony from cover to cover, starting with the story of "From Booker T. To Martin Luther King." When the bus passed by I mumbled, "Bye-bye. I'm going to ride all the way home tonight."

Several shoppers entered the store after five o'clock. Seeing the long check out line, I went to Amanda and whispered, "May I bag the groceries for you?"

"You certainly may," she said. "That would help me out a lot."

Time passed quickly after I began working and talking to Amanda. She taught me how to carefully wrap glass jars, put cartons of eggs on top and make sure that sliced bread didn't get smashed.

After the store closed, Mr. Hamilton put my two heavy bags into the back of his black pickup truck and then locked up the place. I slid into the front seat beside Amanda for the ride home. Having a ride all the way home made me feel like a boulder had been lifted, setting me free to breathe.

"It's been a long week," Mr. Hamilton said. "Thank God for Sunday off."

"Daddy, did you notice that I was busier the last two hours than I'd been all day long?" Amanda said. "Davida helped me bag groceries. You might want to consider hiring a bag boy."

"I'll think about it," he said. There was silence for a long time after that.

To my surprise Mr. Hamilton headed straight for Cashmere Road without asking directions.

"Davida, where do you go to church?" he said. I was surprised he remembered my name and shocked by his question. We hadn't talked at all. Why did he ask me about church?

"I used to go to Holy Cross when my daddy lived with us in Marshall Village. But I haven't been to church since we moved to the country."

"Your mother might want to find a church near where you live now," he said. "It's very important for children to grow up learning what the Bible says."

"We don't live near a church," I said, thinking, Mama didn't go to Holy Cross.

"Well I'm going to pray for God to work it out that your family will find a church home," he said.

"Thank you, sir," I said, staring out the window. "Riding beats walking any day," I thought, as familiar houses and trees looked different.

"Stop at the next driveway," I said as the truck rattled around a bend, past a wooded area. "I live at the bottom of the hill."

"Does the city bus come out this far?" he asked as he pulled into my unpaved driveway and stopped.

"No sir," I said, "The bus turns three miles down the road. That's why I waited for a ride." I got out when he left the driver's seat with the engine running.

"It's almost exactly sixteen miles," he said. "And you were going to bring this food on the bus? It's hard enough walking this distance with nothing to carry."

"I told you I lived a long way," I said.

"I'll be glad to bring you home when you shop at Hamilton's Grocery Store," he said. He removed my bags from the back of his pickup. He handed one bag to

Harry who ran to the truck first and the second to Vera, my helper.

"This is Mr. Hamilton, the owner of the grocery store and that's his daughter Amanda inside the truck," I said. "I know it's too dark to really see their faces, but this is my brother Harry and my sister Vera. We can't thank you enough."

"All this for us, Sis?" Harry asked, holding the bag.

"Yeah," I said. "Thank Mr. Hamilton."

"Thank you!" Harry shouted. "You just don't know how much we appreciate you doing this for us."

"Yes sir! Thank you so much," Vera said. "You saved my sister from walking down that long road with these heavy bags. If I had bus fare I would have—"

"Shhh," I said. "He doesn't want to hear that."

"I don't want to hear that you ever have to do that again," Mr. Hamilton said. "I have two daughters of my own and I would not like them to walk the streets at night. Goodnight." He got in his truck and drove away.

I followed the food inside, feeling proud of Harry for not giving me a hard time when I told him to thank Mr. Hamilton. Maybe my brother does appreciate the work I do around here, I thought.

"Ooooo!" Mama said when I told her about my shopping spree. She asked what made Daddy open the account. I didn't know. But I had a feeling that Mr. Hamilton had talked to him about God, or showed him how a father is supposed to treat his daughters. Whatever the reason, I was glad for the change in my routine. I shopped at that store and helped Amanda every Saturday afternoon until Daddy did something stupid.

Chapter 5

IS CHURCH SUPPOSED TO BE FUN?

THE SCHOOL BUS STOPPED in front of my friend Elaine's house. She got on wearing a red A-line skirt and her usual mischievous smile.

"Good morning everybody!" she said, intentionally disturbing the sleepyheads. Nobody ever responded, but she didn't care.

I shook my head and glanced out the window. A squirrel crawled out on a tree branch and picked a big green Maypop. I stared into his beady eyes as he nibbled on the round fruit in his paws. Seeing him search for food made me feel guilty about cutting down trees for firewood. I never thought of animals having to search elsewhere for a meal.

"My goodness! Why are you looking so sad?" Elaine said, plopping down on the seat next to me. "Do you and that squirrel know each other?"

I glanced at her and then leaned back in my seat as the bus jerked away. "I like you," I said. "You joke about everything. Nothing ever bothers you."

"Well, I try not to let anything get me down," she said.

"I'm sitting here thinking about how I tried to move away from home. but ended up coming back. That squirrel likes where it lives, I guess, and doesn't have to worry about anything or anybody until people like us chop down trees and force them to move."

"You're thinking too hard," she said. "Maybe you can escape the country in your mind. Just do what you have to do until you're grown and old enough to move away like

your big sisters. I forget about home every Sunday while
I'm at church. "

"Hmmm, that's a good idea," I said. "Maybe I'll start
coming to your church and see what's going on there."

"C'mon. I've been telling you to come ever since ya'll
moved out here. We have fun all day long every Sunday,"
she said. "If you're at church, then you won't be bored or
working at home."

"How will I get there?" I said. "Your daddy's car is
already full when he leaves your house."

"Deacon Hamilton picks up people on the back of
his truck every Sunday morning at 8:30. Be standing out
there when that black pickup makes a U-turn at the fork
of the road and all you have to do is climb on back when
he stops."

The conversation with Elaine was fresh on my mind
when I got up early Sunday morning and walked a country
mile to the fork in the road. Several other children whose
parents had no car were already there when I arrived.

"Good morning," I panted. "I'm so glad I didn't miss
the truck."

"Hi, Davida. It's a surprise to see you here," a girl
said. "Don't ya'll have a car?"

"Yeah, they got a Ford," someone answered for me.

"Is this your first time going to Corinthian Baptist,"
someone asked.

"Here they come!" a boy yelled like we were far
away. We lined up side-by-side and faced the street so we
could hop onboard.

I almost panicked when I realized that Deacon
Hamilton was the same man who owned the grocery store
near Daddy's room. No wonder he knew about Cashmere
Road!

Please don't let him tell anybody my business, I
thought.

"Good morning," he said when the truck stopped.
Everybody spoke to him as we climbed on back. He didn't
seem to recognize me. *Perfect!*

That first Sunday morning we talked a lot as the wind whipped through the girls' hair. I learned that Elaine had told most of us about Deacon Hamilton's truck stop.

Most of the members met their relatives every Sunday at Corinthian Baptist Church. Elaine was the only person who knew how bad I felt about my family not going to church at all. That, too, was nobody's business but mine.

As soon as the people saw me on the church grounds they began asking questions.

"Who yo peoples?" an old man asked me.

"She's with me," Elaine answered. "Her family doesn't go to this church."

Even though I didn't ask her to defend me, Elaine gave everybody the same response. I didn't have to say a word. I felt like she was my big sister looking out for me since she was two years older. Elaine was kin to nearly everybody in the church. Her parents, nine siblings, aunts, uncles, and cousins all attended Corinthian Baptist. Her relatives were deacons, deaconesses, ushers, choir members, trustees, the church clerk, and the church secretary. They also voted on decisions about purchasing church property, who would be buried in the church cemetery, who to hire and fire as pastor, how much to pay him, and how much to pay for the church parsonage.

"I know *everything* about this church," Elaine said. "I hear my parents talking church business all the time."

"Well, I know *nothing* about church business," I said.

That first Sunday we spent the entire day and evening at church. The longest part of the service was the third offering. Offering number one was the benevolence (nickel and dime) offering where we passed the pans. During offering number two, we walked around and dropped money in pans on the table. Other offerings followed the march-around offering. I found myself mimicking the deacons who counted at the table. They kept calling for more money.

"We need twenty more dollars; thirteen more dollars; six dollars and forty-four cents more; eight dollars and five cents more…"

"What?" I said. "Why is the last amount higher than before?"

"Cause some of them can't count!" Elaine giggled. "Sometimes they make a mistake. But most of the time it's easier to count whole dollars. It's their job to squeeze as much money out of people's pockets as they can!"

"You are too funny!" I said.

"We'll be here for a singing program with guest churches this afternoon for the mother's annual day," she said, "and then we go to BTU, I mean Baptist Training Union, in the evening."

In closing, we sang, "Blest be the tie that binds our hearts in Christian love," swinging our hands up in the air and down again. The boy next to me squeezed my hand too tight but I bit my bottom lip and endured the pain. After the final "Amen," we hurried outside. We were already in single file lines by the time the women pulled their picnic baskets out of car trunks. Somebody passed back a stack of flimsy paper plates and forks as the line inched forward.

"After we get served here we'll move on over to the next line," Elaine said.

"A lot of chickens sacrificed their lives to feed all these hungry folks today," I said. "No wonder everybody has gospel birds running around in the yard!"

She laughed at me. "Wait till you taste the cakes and pies. They'll bring them out later. You don't want to miss Aunt Hannah's Sock-It-To-Me cake."

I stood behind Elaine when dessert time rolled around. My tummy was full but I wasn't about to miss my special treat. I was in food heaven.

"Now I know why Rev. Taylor said the grace before he dismissed us," I said. "He'd never get people's attention out here!"

"He's already got five or six plates of food himself and people are still bringing him more plates," she said. "His wife won't have to cook all next week."

The day didn't seem so long when good food was being passed around.

That Sunday night, Elaine arranged for me to get a ride back home with one of her cousins who was going in my direction. I squeezed past one woman and sat on the edge of the backseat, wedged between two stout women's thighs. I felt like I had on a girdle that was too tight until one woman was dropped off and I could breathe again.

I ran inside my house with a new attitude that night thinking, "I might be stuck here all week in my body, but my mind is looking forward to Sundays at Corinthian Baptist." I didn't know why it had taken me so long to accept Elaine's invitation, but I knew that was the place I wanted to be every Sunday. I stomped across the living room floor singing the Jubilee Choir's song, "I am bound for the Promised Land, I am bound for the Promised Land, oh who will come and go with me, I am bound for the Promised Land."

"Sis, what's gotten into you?" Harry said.

"Oh, I'm just happy! I had a great time all day long at Corinthian Baptist. We went to Sunday school first, then church. Women served food everywhere. Then we went to a singing program where all the choirs showed out. They sang like they were competing for a prize. People were running all around the church. It was so hot up in that place! Then we went to a group meeting with girls and boys my own age. It was so much fun!"

"You were gone all day long!" he said.

"Yeah! And I loved every minute of it, too! From now on I'm going back every Sunday. You can come, too, if you get up early to catch a ride."

"I'll pass. Sunday morning is the time to sleep late. I'll just listen to the programs on the radio like Mama does." He rushed toward the front door.

"Suit yourself," I hollered. I picked up Andrew, who was crying, and then danced and sang, "Oh, will you come and go with me, I am bound for the Promised Land." He hushed and flashed a faint smile. I placed my cheek against his and rocked him in my arms as I continued to dance. At last, in my mind I had escaped my depressing surroundings and entered an exciting new dimension.

The next Sunday morning I got up early so I could reach the truck stop before Deacon Hamilton arrived at the fork in the road. I climbed on board wondering why I hadn't known about this ride before.

When we parked in the reserved space, the old man I'd seen last week was standing beside a wide wooden post. Flashing his dentures like he was overjoyed to see us, he hobbled over and grabbed my arm as I climbed off the back of the pickup.

"Who yo peoples?" He asked as if my identity had changed since last Sunday.

Elaine showed up while he was talking. "She's with me, Uncle Buddy!" She shouted like he was hard of hearing, then laughed and turned to me. "He's going to ask you that question every time he sees you. He's senile."

"He's your uncle? You must be kin to everybody here."

"Almost, but not quite," she said.

We headed toward the Sunday School building next door to the sanctuary. I felt a lot more comfortable this time because I knew a lot of the children who lived along Cashmere Road. Determined to enjoy every moment of my day, I did just that.

Monday morning on the school bus I told Elaine how much I liked spending the past two Sundays at Corinthian Baptist.

"Then why don't you join and become a member of the junior usher board?" she said. "We have a lot of fun singing, marching, and hanging out together."

"Oh, I don't know."

"Think about it. I guarantee you'll be glad you did."

"Is it okay if I join another church? I think I'm still a member of Holy Cross even though I haven't been there since we moved from Marshall Village five years ago."

"I don't see why not. You can ask that question when you walk the aisle. Somebody will let you know what you have to do."

"Why join if I already feel I belong there?"

"That's just the way it is," she said. "Only members can serve on the usher board."

All week I thought about our conversation and then made up my mind.

Chapter 6
MY NEW LIFE

ON MY THIRD SUNDAY AT CORINTHIAN BAPTIST, Uncle Buddy hobbled over again as soon as Deacon Hamilton parked his pickup.

I looked at Elaine who was standing nearby and mouthed the phrase I expected to hear.

"Who yo peoples?" he said again.

"She's with—" Elaine said before he interrupted her.

"Not you!" he said. "I'm talkin' ta hur." He stared at me, cocked his head to one side and squinted his eyes like he was inspecting me with those black horn-rimmed magnifying glasses propped on his nose. "Whatsa madder wid ya? Da cat done got yo tongue?"

"No sir," I said.

Elaine grabbed my arm and jerked me away. "He's not as senile as I thought," she said. "Dirty old man. He wants to talk to you."

"Uncle Buddy sliced you with his tongue, huh?" I said.

We giggled all the way to Sunday school class. I didn't pay attention to anything the teacher said because my mind raced ahead to worship service. I had decided to walk down the aisle and join no matter what the pastor preached.

After class, while on our way to the sanctuary, Elaine and I chatted until a little-bitty usher, dressed in a navy blue uniform, lifted her white-gloved hand and flashed a stern look that could kill a flitting fly. Her gaze commanded attention and she got it, too.

The congregation sang "Nearer My God to Thee" while Elaine slid into a wooden pew near the back. I sat next to her thinking we were close enough to the fire that spews out of the pastor's mouth without getting burned.

"Jesus went to Calvary, ha!" Rev. Taylor shouted like he was in pain. "To save a sinner like you and me! Ha! That's good news, children! Ha! That's good news! Amen!"

Why did he keep saying "ha?" It was scary to think that he might choke on his "ha" in front of us and nobody would notice until it was too late.

Rev. Taylor quit shouting, came off the platform and said in a normal voice, "The door of the church is open."

That was my cue. I got up and rushed forward. Everybody clapped just like the people had done at Holy Cross Church when I walked the aisle at seven years old. It felt so good to be the person getting so much attention.

How I wish my mama could see me now.

A deacon told me to sit in one of the metal folding chairs the male ushers had placed at the front of the church facing the congregation. When I sat down, I saw little children, teenagers, grownups and old folks coming from different ends of the long pews. Twelve people in all came forward. The ushers kept on bringing chairs without anybody saying a word. I wished Harry could be there to see the men at work.

A woman, the church clerk, startled me when she leaned over and asked, "What's your name?

"Davida Kincaid," I said. She'd caught me thinking how different my life would be if Daddy had been a preacher, a deacon, or an usher.

"Do you want to be baptized?" she said while writing my name.

"I got baptized when I was seven."

"You can join by baptism, by letter from your old church, or on Christian experience," she said. "I'll just check Christian experience. That's the fastest way to become a member. Please stand."

I stood up, feeling nervous in front of so many people.

She stood beside me, touched my arm, and said, "We have Davida Kincaid coming to unite with the church on Christian experience."

Deacon Hamilton asked, "Church, shall we accept this young lady on Christian experience? All in favor signify by saying, aye."

I got scared. What if they reject me? I don't have any family here to vote for me. I felt self-conscious, like a piece of trash that somebody had tossed at a garbage can and missed. I wasn't supposed to be standing in front of those people any more than that trash was supposed to be on the ground. What if they don't want me to join their church? I'd be embarrassed if they voted no. A drumroll played in my mind. Then loud "ayes" from hundreds of Negroes all over the sanctuary tickled my ears.

Whew! What a relief! They accepted me! Tears sprang from my eyes just as a female usher handed me a Kleenex.

"Opposers, nay. The ayes have it," Deacon Hamilton said without waiting for a response.

Rev. Taylor took my hand in his and said, "Welcome. With this right hand of fellowship I give you all the rights and privileges of every other member of Corinthian Baptist Church." His big fat hand squeezed my fingers tight enough to hurt my knuckles. I was too happy to let a slight pain bother me.

Still wiping my eyes, I returned to my seat.

Elaine stood up and hugged me. "Now you really are my sister. We're sisters in the Lord."

"I'm a member because of you." She had no idea how good it felt to be accepted by a bunch of strangers after my own daddy had abandoned me.

After the benediction, I stepped outside wondering if the junior usher board would accept me, too. Uncle Buddy was waiting at the door. "Now ya blongst to da church. Youse one o us now," he said. His loose dentures looked like they could drop out at any moment. He was still talking when a woman wrapped her arms around me, smothering my face between her huge breasts before I could say a word.

"Welcome, welcome, welcome!" she said. "We look forward to you joining us. I'm Sister Jenkins, president of the junior usher board."

I couldn't breathe until she released me. Her warm and fluffy hug had made me feel like I had a new mama in my new church family.

"Thank you," I said, wondering if Elaine had told her I wanted to be an usher.

Two weeks later I had on a black pleated skirt and white blouse like all the other junior ushers. It was our Sunday to serve the Lord. I stood in line behind Elaine waiting for our turn to march around the offering pan when she looked over her shoulder and whispered, "Don't worry if you don't give any money." She wore her familiar mischievous grin. "God is pleased when we show up and show out with our song and dance if that's all we've got to give. He knows you don't have a job."

I nodded. I had a coin to give because I would have been embarrassed to make that grand march and not give something.

We started out on the left foot as usual, but I didn't know why. I watched Elaine step out and then it was my turn. We were in motion singing and swaying to the tune, "You can't beat God giving, no matter how you try." The organ music gave me chill bumps. It was different from the radio music we listened to everyday. I was glad to drop my nickel in the sterling silver pan that announced the offerings with a loud *Clink! Clink! Clink!* in tune with our rhythm.

Proud to belong to the church, I smiled and held my head high as we marched through the aisles singing. We rocked to the left and to the right, and swayed back and forth swinging white-gloved hands. I floated on my feet as I moved to the drumbeat.

***

One Sunday when we weren't ushering, I followed Elaine past the offering pan in front of the pulpit and walked straight out the door.

"It's so cool how my life has changed since I started attending church," I said. "I wish I'd come sooner."

"Well, you're here now and that's all that matters," she said as we walked toward the girls and cute boys who were already gathered in their favorite meeting spot.

It was okay for us to go outside, but everybody knew not to leave the church grounds. The old folks would not let us escape the Word. We could still hear everything that went on inside. Rev. Taylor whooped, hollered and gasped for breath while the adults shouted and screamed like they were cheerleaders on a football field.

"It's too stressful watching Rev. Taylor choke himself almost to death," I said.

"Didn't your other pastor preach the same way?" Elaine said.

"No, he started singing when he was almost finished preaching."

"Oh, that's called 'tuning,'" she said. "Everybody sing yesssss."

With heads tilted back, everybody except me sang, "Yessssss!"

I laughed. "One thing that really stands out at both churches is that deacons pray long prayers that they must have memorized. They say the same thing every Sunday and even put emphasis on the same words."

"You noticed that too, huh?" said a tall thin boy named Ullysses Jr. "We all know Deac Hamilton's prayer word-for-word even though he says it fresh every Sunday. You want to hear me say it?"

"Naw U-2," Elaine said, calling him by his nickname. "Once is enough for one day."

Everybody laughed. She was always quick with the tongue.

We stood outside talking to boys who liked to entertain us with "yo mama" jokes. Elaine knew most of the right answers because she had seven brothers who were jokesters.

"Why did the farmer take yo mama all over his garden?" U-2 said.

Elaine didn't know that answer. We tried to guess the answer but finally gave up.

"Because she was his hoe!" he said. He stomped into the middle of our little circle swaying like Godzilla on the move and pounded his chest.

"Watch out now," Elaine said. "Don't let one joke cause you to get the bighead."

The church doors swung open and people began pouring outside. U-2 spotted his grandma coming down the steps.

"See ya!" He pushed through the circle and ran toward her.

The rest of the teenagers scattered like roaches do when somebody turns on the light. They went to meet their parents at the bottom of the steps or to the family car. I stayed close to Elaine so I could get my meal and a ride home with one of her relatives.

That evening at Baptist Training Union (BTU) the teacher said, "Church life can become so ritualistic or mundane on the one hand, or so activity-centered on the other hand that it becomes boring or exciting to the extent that a person can forget the real purpose for coming altogether." Then she called on me to read our Bible lesson found in Mark 7:5-7 and Isaiah 29:13.

So the Pharisees and teachers of religious law asked him, "Why don't your disciples follow our age-old tradition? They eat without first performing the hand-washing ceremony."

Jesus answered them, "How right Isaiah was when he prophesied about you! You are hypocrites, just as he wrote, 'These people claim to worship me, but their words are meaningless, and their hearts are somewhere else. Their religion is nothing but human rules and traditions, which they have simply memorized'."

When I finished reading, the teacher said, "Remember last week's lesson about how Jesus overturned the tables of the moneychangers in the temple. The church is supposed to be a house of prayer so he was angry that those people had turned it into a den of thieves. He wants you, and me, to be real in our worship and real in our service."

Oops! We just talked about saying memorized prayers and churches doing the same old thing everywhere. We were at church today but not in church for the sermon. Was I a hypocrite? I dared not look up at my classmates, but I think they had the same thoughts I had because it was mighty quiet in that room of 19 teenagers.

Gosh, words can have a powerful effect.

Questions jammed my mind. We never washed our hands before eating after church. All we did was jump in the serving lines before they got too long. What about the grownups? Are they hypocrites for skipping Sunday School and BTU? They only have two or three people in their class. Don't adults have to study the Bible, too? They only go to eleven o'clock worship service and afternoon singing programs, unless there's a revival.

Could the pastor be a hypocrite too? One day I walked to Sunday School because I missed my ride on the pick up. The only person who drove past me on the way to church was Rev. Taylor with a long cigar sticking out of his mouth. He had both hands on the steering wheel of the long black Cadillac that Elaine said the church provided for him. I wondered why he didn't stop to give me a ride. He said he knew all the members. So he must have known that I was on my way to Sunday School. Is he a hypocrite for smoking a cigar after he told us not to defile our temple, which is the Lord's?

I kept my head down so nobody would notice how guilty I felt.

After class, Elaine and I talked as we headed outside.

"I came to church for Sunday entertainment, but that BTU lesson really made me think," I said. "I feel like a hypocrite."

"Me too," she giggled. "But don't worry. Whatever you're feeling now will be gone by next Sunday."

"Girl, I'm serious."

"I am, too. Don't you forget Rev. Taylor's sermon before church is dismissed? That's just the way it is. That's why we have to hear a new sermon every Sunday."

Chapter 7
GROWING PAINS

"GET OFF ME!" I YELLED and jumped off the rollaway. I flicked the light switch and saw millions of bedbugs crawl every which way as I slapped them away from my neck and shoulders. How did they get in my rollaway? Why did they always bother me?

My fingers squeezed the ones I caught on the bed. I wanted revenge. "You're a bunch of hypocrites! You were big and bad in the dark. Why run away in the light?" It was disgusting to see a white sheet speckled with my blood that oozed out of them. "That'll teach you not to bother me."

I stared down at the sheet, angry because most of the bugs escaped. I knew they'd return as soon as I got back in the bed, so I shook out my sheet and pillowcase and carried them to a pleather chair that matched the sofa where bedbugs liked to hide. I got a wooden chair out of the kitchen to use as a footstool. With the pillow propped behind my head as a cushion from the sheetrock wall, I spent the rest of the night half sitting up.

To avoid bedbugs, I slept in the chair again the next night because we were out of Hot Shot spray. I fell asleep but later jumped off the chair, slapping crawling critters off my chest. I knew before I turned on the light they'd found me. The bedbugs disappeared into the chair but left fresh bloodstains on my pajama top. I had to find another place to sleep.

"They must smell me a mile away," I said. "What now? I can't lose another night's sleep."

I grabbed my pillow, and went out on the front porch. It was warm enough to stay outside. Bedbugs can't hide in a metal chair. I spread a wool Army blanket over the rusty swing to cover the holes and provide padding so I could stretch out. I put a sheet on top of the blanket to keep it from making me itch and laid my feather pillow on one end of the swing. Then I lay on my side between the folded sheet with my back against the back of the chair and my head toward the woods. From that position I could see anybody who came on the porch or out the front door.

It was quiet, except for the sound of chirping crickets somewhere out in early morning darkness. I woke up that morning feeling rested. I'd found my bug-free bed.

On the third night of sleeping outdoors, I heard a rustling sound in the grass. I opened my eyes slowly, afraid of what I might see. In the early morning light I saw a snake slither through the grass toward the front porch. Afraid it might come to get me, I froze, pondering what I should do.

If I scream, it might crawl up on the porch to get away, I thought. Then where would I run?

I remembered when I was nine and a snake came in our kitchen and Grandpa Cox killed it. Mama had said, "When you see one snake, there's a nest of them some-where nearby." That thought frightened me. I sat up with my knees tucked safely beneath my chin. My heart doubled the average of one hundred beats per minute as I watched that green critter slither past the porch to the other side. When it was out of sight, I dashed through the front door.

"Mama, there's a snake out in the yard!" I cried.

"We've got to kill it!" she hollered from the kitchen.

"We? Not me!" "We" must mean my other brave self, I thought. Bedbugs? Yes. Snakes? No.

Mama ran outside and grabbed the garden hoe that we kept at the corner of the house.

I watched her through the window, chopping that snake like she was chopping firewood. Pieces of the snake wiggled around like it didn't know how to die.

"Why won't it die?" I yelled.

"It's a joint snake," Mama said. "I have to find the head!" She walked around searching and then turned the hoe upside down and slammed it on the ground.

"Hallelujah!" I shouted.

Harry ran into the living room and stared out the window. I told him what happened as the two of us rushed outside and watched Mama pick up the scattered pieces with the hoe. She tossed them into the woods and then returned saying, "I got too many children 'round here to have a snake in the yard."

We clapped for our brave mama. She knew she had to be strong because Grandpa Cox couldn't help us this time. He died two years ago.

"I saw you go, whack, whack, whack!" I shouted. I swung my arms like I had a hoe in my hand. "I was thinking, 'You go Mama!' I am so proud of you! That ole snake didn't scare you!"

"Why didn't you call me?" Harry said. "I would have killed it like Grandpa did."

"Was I supposed to say, 'Wait right here Mr. Snake while I go wake up my son so he can come and kill you?'" Mama said.

We all laughed, Mama included.

"How did you know you had to find the head?" I said.

"A joint snake is like a freight train," Mama said. "As soon as you hit it, the car boxes fall apart."

That's baloney! I thought. It sounded like another one of Mama's old wives tales. But it bothered me that the pieces kept on moving.

That same day at school, I went to the library and looked up joint snakes. I learned that Mama was right. The glass lizard (also called a glass snake or joint snake) had a habit of breaking its tail into many pieces resembling shattered glass. When threatened, the pieces continue wiggling to distract a predator while the glass lizard makes its escape. Then it grows another tail.

I marveled at Mama's knowledge and bravery. She was much more confident and courageous than she was when her papa was alive. Mama was now grown and on her own.

"Wow!" I muttered. "When I grow up I'm going to get as far away from the country as possible. I don't want anything growing around my house but grass."

Mama's saying, "If it ain't one thing it's another," proved true.

After the bedbugs and snake, came mosquitoes. I did my best to protect myself, but they attacked me all during summer break. Since girls weren't allowed to wear pants to school, I wore knee high socks to prevent bites and to hide my blotchy skin, even in hot weather. What a way to start ninth grade.

One night I sat on the sofa rubbing my itchy legs and wondering why I was the only one in my family who always got bitten.

"Mama, why do things like biting me so much?" I said.

Mama stopped to look at my legs as though for the first time.

"Mosquitoes just like some people more than others," she said. "Like me, bee stings make me swell up all over. Ya'll just get a red bump when they sting you. Remember to rub. Don't scratch or you'll make it worse."

Scratching provided more relief than rubbing, but the more I scratched around the bumps, the more they itched and then turned into ugly sores. Covering them with long socks didn't help because sometimes I ended up pulling off the scab.

In the school library I found out why they attacked me: Mosquitoes are attracted to carbon dioxide in the breath and they can detect it from miles away. When the female—the only bloodsucker—gets close she makes her final choice based on skin temperature, odor, other chemicals or whatever pleases its eyes. If people are outside together, one person will usually get most of the bites.

At last I understood. I couldn't find a way to make them stay away from me, but I continued reading and learned that when mosquitoes bite they inject chemicals to keep the blood from clotting and reduce pain. The chemicals cause irritation.

"Well what do you know!" I murmured. The mosquito applies anesthesia before sucking the innocent victim's blood. They sneak up on people and prick without warning.

I closed the thick encyclopedia, leaned back in the chair and stared at the name Britannica on the cover. Being informed felt good. I related what I'd read about mosquitoes to myself. Uncovering scars, flaws, and blemishes when I removed my long socks was like exposing bad habits, lies, character defects, a quick temper, and... whatever. Seeing the truth can be very unsightly and removing a comfortable covering can be downright painful. Yet, letting go of scars, releasing anything that hinders a healthy self-image, can be a liberating experience.

"I'm tired of covering up. I'll just have to be myself, show my scars and suffer the consequences so I can be healed." As soon as I muttered those words I thought about the 1 John 1:9 Bible verse Rev. Taylor quoted every Sunday, "If we confess our sins, God is faithful and just to forgive us our sins and to cleanse us from all unrighteousness."

Mama's papa put it this way, "When ya empty da junk dat's buried deep down inside ya, den God kin fill da empty space wid all da good stuff he got in store for ya."

Only God knew the other shameful thing I'd covered up for years. One day I planned to tell everybody how much worse off my family was in the country than we were when we lived in the city. Too bad a family can't choose where to be poor.

I hated our living conditions out in the woods but nothing seemed to bother Mama. I never saw her cry and seldom heard her complain about anything.

"We have to take what we get in this life," she said. "We gotta live 'til we die."

Mama killing that snake surprised me like all the babies she had brought home.

"You can't read a person's mind," she liked to say.

I think she read my mind and decided to trick me into doing her a big favor that I would never have done had she told me the truth.

Chapter 8

UNUSUAL VOICES

MRS. BELL, MY NINTH GRADE English teacher, asked six students and me to participate in an intramural competition. The winner would represent Dover Junior High in its first district-wide oratorical contest. Excited about the chance to compete, I memorized "The Bridge Builder" by Will Allen Dromgoole, a poem about an old man who built a bridge to make the journey easier for any young man that would come after him, and "Young Fellow My Lad" by Robert William Service, about a father who longed to hear from his son that had gone away to fight in a war.

Both poems were touching to me because they featured men who cared about children. Why couldn't my daddy be like one of those men? It was hard to choose between them so I asked my teacher for help.

"They are both beautiful," she said. "Whichever one you feel most comfortable presenting will be fine. The choice is yours."

After several weeks of practicing both, I decided to polish my delivery of the poem that described a father longing in vain for his missing son. It was perfect. For years, I'd longed in vain for my daddy to come back home.

On the day before our school competition, I stood in front of the class and presented my speech. Oh, I couldn't believe it when the whole class gave me a standing ovation. Yeah! I was on my way to getting my first trophy.

"Davida is clearly the frontrunner in this competition," Mrs. Bell announced to our ninth grade class. "I believe she will represent us exceptionally well."

"She'd better get her hair done," I heard a girl whisper.

My classmates snickered.

I pretended not to hear. They're just jealous, I thought.

"Shouldn't a boy say that poem?" A boy said. "Are you going to dress up like a man? How will you disguise your itty-bitty voice?"

I dropped my head. The questions were about me, not my speech. I hadn't thought about what I would wear. I opened my mouth to answer, but all I said was "I⌐⌐—" before Mrs. Bell interrupted me.

"We believe she will be victorious in the oratorical contest," she said. "Don't we, Davida?"

"Yes ma'am," I said. "We will win."

"Good. Then hold your head up. Class, give her one more round of applause while she returns to her seat."

"I'm a champion," I thought. I can't disappoint them, and I won't.

"Thank you," Mrs. Bell said. "Now let's continue reading Hamlet."

As a student read aloud, I sat thinking more about the negative comments than the applause and praise I had just received from my classmates and teacher.

After class, Mrs. Bell called me over to her desk and gave me some practice tips. "Look straight at each judge's nose or forehead. They will think you are giving them good eye contact. Make sure you move your head in different directions. Remember to make hand gestures as you speak, and watch your intonations. We will practice every day until the district competition."

During my lunchtime practice sessions, I worked hard to demonstrate everything Mrs. Bell had taught me. I wanted to please my teacher.

I could count on Mrs. Bell to say, "Wonderful! Excellent! Do it that way at the competition!" Her positive affirmations showed me that she cared about how I felt and the delivery of my speech. Even when I messed up in practice – and I did at least once each day – she'd say, "Start over. I know you can do better than that."

"I'm sorry," I said. "I know this poem. I don't know why I forgot that line." I did not want to disappoint my teacher and make her regret choosing me.

"That's all right," she said, you'll get it right the next time."

"Tomorrow is your big day," she said on the last day of practice. "Recite your poem for me just one more time."

I delivered my flawless speech feeling confident that I would win the competition. When I finished, Mrs. Bell showed all thirty-two teeth, stood up behind her desk and clapped.

"Do that tomorrow and you'll bring home the first place trophy," she said.

I beamed like a flashlight in the woods. I believed her. Singing with the junior usher board at church had helped to build my confidence in standing in front of people. I pictured myself coming back to Dover Junior High the day after the contest struggling beneath the weight of the biggest first place trophy anyone had ever seen.

The following morning I woke up around six o'clock. I sprang off the rollaway to get ready for the oratorical contest. The school bus would come around six-thirty and I couldn't miss it. I had to hurry up.

I rushed into Mama's bedroom and pulled open the chifforobe door to get my dress. That's all I remember until I heard Mama's voice.

"Davida! Davida!"

She sounded far away. Then I smelled the strong odor of camphor and turned my head. I coughed and opened my eyes. My mama was kneeling beside me, her face close to mine.

Old Miss Crockett, the neighbor who lived back in the woods and sold home brew, was leaning over me moving an open bottle back and forth beneath my nose.

"She's coming to!" she said. Spit dripped in my face from the gap in her bottom front teeth. I stared at her, wondering why she was in our house. She'd never been there before.

I started to jump up when I realized I was lying flat on my back in front of the chifforobe. I needed to get dressed in a hurry. Both Mama and Miss Crockett grabbed one of my arms and pulled me to my feet.

"What happened?" I asked. They helped me get off the floor and sat me down on the edge of Mama's bed.

"You fainted," Mama said.

"What! Oh no! I've got to hurry to catch the bus. I'm not even dressed yet." I started to stand up, but Mama pushed my shoulders down.

"The school bus is already gone. You been out cold for a long time," Mama said. "I sent Harry to get Miss Crockett to come help 'cause you scared me."

I groaned and threw both hands up in the air as I sank backward onto mama's bed. "All that hard work for nothing!" I cried. I lay there thinking about missing the oratorical contest. Something moved under my back and I popped up off Mama's baby wiggling beneath the covers and leaned forward, my face in my hands.

Sharp cramps in my stomach got my attention. I'd been so busy rehearsing my speech that I'd forgotten that I get lightheaded every time my period starts.

"Why me?" I cried.

"What are you crying about?" Mama asked.

"I don't know what to tell my teacher," I said. "She worked so hard to prepare me for today's speech competition."

"Tell her you fainted and missed the bus," Mama said. "Let her know the school bus is your only way out of this place in the mornings.

"She doesn't want to hear that," I said. "She wants to hear that I won a trophy."

"Well if you can't tell her the truth," Mama said, "then make up a lie."

She and Miss Crockett left the room.

I spent most of the day asking God why I fainted on the day of the competition. Why not the day before or the day after? If we had a car I still could have gone to school. If we lived near a bus stop I could have gone, too. But no, this day, out of three hundred sixty-five days in a year, I was stuck at home because I had no control over when my period would start and how my body would respond.

Angry about attacks from an invisible enemy, I slapped my thighs. "I missed a great opportunity to show everybody how bold I can be. Life, you're a real party pooper."

I decided to go and apologize to Mrs. Bell before class the next morning. All the way to school I imagined her disappointment. She probably thought I'd gotten stage fright but I was too embarrassed to tell her the real reason why I missed the competition. I wanted her to know that I was sorry about what happened.

The moment I stepped into English class the next morning, before I could say a word, Mrs. Bell said, "I am so sorry you missed the speech competition yesterday. I'm certain you would have won."

"I really wanted to come, but I just couldn't," I said, looking into my disappointed teacher's eyes. Then I sat down, thinking, "Why didn't you call my house?" But then I realized I wouldn't have wanted her to come for me and see where I live. And there was no way I could tell her that I'd missed the school bus because I fainted. Who would believe that fainting and starting a period were related? She'd think I was crazy.

Bertha Nell, a tall skinny girl seated beside me in the front row, glanced over at me and burst into loud laughter. She acted as if she'd suddenly heard a funny joke.

"What is it that you find so comical?" Mrs. Bell asked her.

I was shocked when Bertha Nell laughed louder and pointed to the bridge of my nose. She drew attention to what Mama called, "the Cherokee Indian in me."

"Her nose is shaped so funny," she said. "It has a big hump in it like a chicken butt!"

My classmates laughed and stared at my nose.

I leaned over and breathed a seething, "Drop dead!"

Mrs. Bell blushed. She was stunned by Bertha Nell's candid response.

"Turn to Shakespeare's Midsummer Night's Dream in your literature book," she said. "Bertha Nell has clearly forgotten that people have feelings. Let's see if we can learn something about genuine love and how to treat others as you would like to be treated."

So much for my big day of receiving accolades for winning the oratorical contest, I thought. I'll have to look for another opportunity to make a lasting impression on my classmates.

Three weeks later the very first ninth grade graduating class of Dover Junior High met to consider the class gift. We voted to bequeath an Anthology of Songs to our beloved school before leaving for Madison High.

Grateful for another chance to leave a legacy, I chose to sing my favorite song, "Two Lovers" by Mary Wells, even though I knew I had trouble carrying a tune. I thought the song lyrics were perfect because I was torn between wanting to stay at my familiar junior high where all the teachers liked me, and moving on to the unknown.

At the first class rehearsal, I stood on stage and sang my solo with the record playing in the background behind the school curtain. I thought I sounded okay.

When I sat down, someone tapped me on my shoulder. I turned and saw Sylvia and Nancy, two girls I didn't know very well.

"May we sing backup for you," Sylvia whispered, pointing to Nancy.

"Why not sing your own song?" I said.

"We're too shy to sing in front of our classmates," Sylvia said.

"Then, okay. I'll sing the verses and you sing the chorus."

The three of us agreed to play the song in the background, too.

At the second stage rehearsal, my group, The Wellettes, rehearsed the entire song. I felt pretty good about our performance as we sat listening to others.

Preparing for the historic day was fun. Every ninth grader was required to participate in some way, and there was no shortage of talent. We had ballet and tap dancers, a clown, a juggler, a magician, a ventriloquist, a preacher, a comedienne, soloists, duets, trios, quartets and quintets.

We even had two girls walking around passing out a basketful of handmade crepe paper hearts containing the words, "Dover's first graduating class is the best. We paved the way for all the rest. Love, Class No. 1." That was the message in The Bridge Builder poem.

I was enjoying myself as a spectator when Velma, a girl in my Civics class, leaned forward from the seat behind me and interrupted the Tempters rendition of the Temptations' "My Girl."

"Why don't you let Sylvia sing lead?" Velma whispered. "She already leads the youth choir at her church."

I turned around and whispered, "Then let her sing her own song!"

She had a lot of nerve dipping in my Kool-Aid. Busybody! I thought about Bertha Nell making a comment about my nose. What's wrong with people anyhow? Don't they think before they open their mouths? Instead of enjoying the show, her mind was somewhere else.

I turned my attention back to the performance but I sat there feeling annoyed for being interrupted. Just because she wasn't paying attention to the Tempters' performance didn't give her the right to distract me. What makes people think they're not supposed to pay attention at rehearsal?

She can't imagine how much courage it took for me to agree to sing in front of the student body. I wondered how she'd feel if I'd asked her, "Why don't you let somebody else dress up like a rabbit and do your bunny hop?" People need confidence and compliments at rehearsal, not criticism. Even if she thought she was being helpful, her timing made me suspicious because Sylvia was seated right beside her. I wondered which of them came up with the idea of a new lead singer.

It's amazing how people seldom notice you until you try to do something. Then they want to add their two cents worth.

At the next rehearsal Velma's comment prompted me to listen to Sylvia's soprano voice behind me. Her singing, like Minnie Rippleton's, soothed the listeners' ears— including mine. After rehearsal, I talked to her privately.

"Would you like to sing lead?" I asked.

"No, I told you I'm too shy," she said.

I felt brave seeing Sylvia's fear. My sister Beverly's constant criticism of everything I did had made me determined not to allow any negative comment to discourage me.

The Talent Showcase was awesome. The entire school, including Bertha Nell, said how much they enjoyed our performance. I knew that our success had a lot to do with Sylvia's voice. Having her in the trio motivated me to perfect my lead. I had fun working with students who did what they had agreed to do. Unlike some other groups that fell apart, clear communication gave us one voice.

Something soon happened that made me wish I had as clear an understanding of my role at home as I had with the Wellettes at school.

Chapter 9

SURPRISE! SURPRISE!

MY MAMA NEVER LOST HER cute figure and good looks. In spite of having a house full of children, she attracted more attention from males than I did, especially when she swished her wide hips. At fifteen, I was just her skinny daughter who had boys for friends, but no boyfriend. Even the white insurance collector who came every other week carrying his big black book was happy to see Mama's rump.

One Thursday afternoon I came out of the kitchen and saw him standing on the porch with his face and both hands pressed against the screen door. He was grinning like he was watching Lucille Ball. His eyes followed Mama's booty as she went into her bedroom.

Dirty old man!

When he saw me staring at him, he cleared his throat and stood up straight.

Drunk Mr. Fred, Mama's boyfriend for many years, had stopped coming to our house. I didn't know what happened to him and didn't care. He was gone and no other man came to spend the weekend. I didn't dare think of him for fear he might return.

When male friends stopped by, Mama went for a ride or just sat in the car with them. Maybe she, too, was ashamed of our house.

One Monday, Mama didn't come home from work. I thought it was just another time when she had missed the last bus to the country and couldn't get a ride.

At bedtime I told Vera, "I need you to stay home and watch Carrie and Andrew if Mama's not here in the morning." I wanted my perfect attendance certificate, but

I knew Vera could miss any day because her bad grades proved that she didn't like school. It baffled me that some students get up early and go to school when they could stay in the bed, sleep all day, and make the same grades.

"Well, all right," Vera giggled. "I get to sleep late tomorrow."

I left home the next morning feeling a little worried but tried not to show it. While at school, I prayed Mama would be at home when I arrived. She wasn't.

"Did Mama call?" I asked Vera.

"No, nobody called here," she said.

I kept wondering where Mama could be as I cooked dinner. That night we played a guessing game of Who Touched Me? Whoever was It wore a blindfold until she named the right person. Around nine o'clock, I realized Mama might not come home again.

"April, I need you to stay home tomorrow to look after Carrie and Andrew," I said. "I don't want Vera to miss her free school lunch again even though she won't mind."

"You know me," Vera said, laughing.

"When's Mama coming home?" April asked. Her voice trembled.

"I really don't know," I said. "I just know that I need you to stay home just in case Mama's not here in the morning."

"Is Mama all right?" Barbara Jean said.

I looked into her big brown eyes and then looked around at all the children. They looked scared.

"Let's pray," I said, reaching for their hands. We formed a circle and they bowed their heads while I talked. "God, we don't know where Mama is, but we ask you to keep her safe and send her back home. You know she's all we have since Daddy left us. So, please hurry up and answer this prayer. In Jesus' name, Amen."

"Group hug!" I said, knowing how much we all needed it. Then they got ready for bed.

I tucked the covers around Carrie and Andrew's neck as I crawled into Mama's bed with them. I lay in the dark room thinking, "What would happen to us if something bad happens to Mama?" I put that thought out of my mind and started counting sheep. *One, two, three…*

I woke up Wednesday morning quite concerned, but tried to act normal. Everybody except April got dressed for school. I felt bad about catching my school bus first and leaving them behind, but I had no choice. "Davida, these are not your children," I reminded myself. All day at school I walked around wishing and praying for Mama.

"You've been gone long enough to scare us," I mumbled.

Mama was at home when I arrived that afternoon.

"Mama, where have you been?" I shouted the moment I walked in and saw her sitting in the living room. "We were worried about you."

"Well, I'm here now," she said like I had no reason to ask questions. She never told us where she'd been and I was too glad to have her back to ask again.

Drunk Mr. Fred surprised me when he showed up on Friday night. He hadn't come in a long time. His driver didn't speed away as usual after dropping him off. Instead, he stayed in the car with the engine running. Mama went out to the driveway and talked to him through the window.

"I hope she tells him to go home and never come back," I mumbled, smiling as I anticipated his reaction if indeed Mama did say that.

I was chanting, "Go home, go home…" when Mama rushed in a few minutes later and removed a sealed envelope tucked inside the big leather Bible on the coffee table where she hid important papers. I glanced at her then back outside. "Why aren't they leaving?" I asked myself just before Mama interrupted my thoughts.

"Davida, I need you to ride downtown with Fred to pick up a package for me," Mama said, handing me the sealed envelope.

"What is it?" I asked.

"You'll see when you get it," she said. "Give this note to the woman sitting at a lil' window just inside the door. Hurry, they're waiting for you."

I ran out and hopped in the blue Buick behind disgusting old Mr. Fred. The two men on the front seat talked to each other while I listened to loud music on the radio. All the way to the hospital I kept wondering what the mysterious package could be.

Does Drunk Mr. Fred know what it is? Why didn't Mama come to pick up her own package? This must be important.

The car stopped next to the curb in front of the Columbia Hospital.

"The hospital! Why are we here? Is Mama sick?" I said.

"She want you to go pick up a package for her," Drunk Mr. Fred slobbered.

I jumped out of the car feeling thoroughly con-fused.

"We'll wait right here," Mr. Fred said. I left them in the car while I walked toward the double glass doors that all patients entered. I knew that hospital very well because I'd been there many times to visit my sister Zenobia before she died.

I spotted the little window with a woman seated behind it. She saw me enter and said, "May I help you?"

"I came to pick up a package for Blossom Kincaid," I said, handing her Mama's sealed envelope. She opened it, read, and then stared at me for a moment. I wondered if she could understand Mama's misspelled words, but I didn't say anything.

"Wait here," she said. "It will take me a few minutes."

The wait was much longer than I'd expected. I paced the tiled floor and watched as people entered and left through the double doors. Finally, the woman returned and said, "Just a few more minutes."

"Thank you." I stepped away from the window wondering what was wrong with Mama. Why was the pharmacist taking so long to fill her prescription?

"Over there," I heard the receptionist say. I looked up and saw a nurse dressed in all white coming toward me carrying a bundle wrapped in a pink receiving blanket. "Blossom Kincaid's baby girl," she said, handing me the bundle and a bag of supplies.

"A baby!" I gasped, and managed not to scream when she showed me the tiny wristband with the handwritten name, Bonnie Kincaid.

"No wonder Mama didn't tell me," I blurted.

"What?" the nurse asked.

"Never mind," I said as I took the surprise pack-age and rushed outside. I needed fresh air on that cool December evening. I felt like a fool after all my speculations. A seventeenth baby never crossed my mind. Prescriptions would have been better. For three days I'd been concerned about Mama's safety while she was in the hospital having a baby. That's all. I laughed to keep from crying.

Mr. Fred saw me coming and opened the car's rear door. I plopped down and placed Bonnie across my lap. I didn't want to touch her, but I had no choice. As the driver pulled away I got the courage to speak up.

"Mr. Fred, did you know what the package was?"

He laughed and said, "Yo Mama told me not to tell ya."

"This is not funny!" I said. It was a long, quiet ride home with a sleeping light-skinned baby on my lap. I sulked all the way. Mama had tricked me. She knew I never would have come to pick up a baby. While Mr. Fred and the driver talked to each other, my mind traveled into the future. One day I'm going to get away from all this, I thought. I'm tired of these babies coming into our house with no daddy.

As soon as the car came to a complete stop, I was ready to jump out, but I had to wait until Mr. Fred opened the door for me. The car drove away as I ran toward the house with Mama's package. I figured he knew I was angry about the surprise.

"Good!" I said. "Go and stay gone!"

Mama met me at the door and I shoved the package into her arms. A voice inside me shouted, "Speak or explode!" I chose to dump my thoughts on her and save myself.

"When will you stop having babies?" I yelled. "I am soooo tired of taking care of your children! We can't even feed the people who already live in this house and now we have to make room for another baby!"

"You can't stop a growing baby," Mama said. "Abortion is wrong as killing somebody."

"Isn't it wrong to have sex when you're not married?!" I said.

Mama said nothing. She carried the baby into her bedroom and laid her on the bed. Then she went to the kitchen and put a pot of water on the stove. She made baby formula with the can of Carnation cream from the bag of supplies the nurse had given me.

After moping around all evening, I ended up laughing at myself to keep from crying as I lay in bed that night. I heard Bonnie crying on the other side of Mama's bedroom door and felt guilty for disliking her. She didn't ask to come into the world or to be in our family. None of us did. Mama could have aborted me, but she didn't. I felt ashamed for talking to my mama the way I had done.

My ear popped as tears rolled into it.

"God, when will the babies stop coming?" I said. "That's all I want to know. Oh, and why do some people wear maternity clothes, but not my mama?"

Chapter 10

THE BABY GIVEAWAY

UNLIKE ANDREW WHO NEEDED constant attention when he was a baby, Bonnie was a happy child who seldom cried. Everybody liked to tickle her so she'd squeal with laughter. Like the joy of Christmas morning, she brought excitement to our house.

One day after Bonnie had just begun walking and getting into everything, I rode home with Uncle Clyde who went to pick up his chainsaw. Since my uncle planned to go right back to the country to cut down a big tree, I carried Bonnie with me so his wife, Aunt Judy, could see our happy baby.

"Pine trees attract lightning," Uncle Clyde said. "I need to cut that tree down 'cause it's too close to the house for comfort." He hurried toward the outdoor shed in his backyard.

"C'mon and have a piece of pound cake while you wait for Clyde," Aunt Judy said.

"This is Bonnie, Mama's baby," I said.

"She's a 'lil cutie pie," Aunt Judy said. She removed the see-through lid off the cake stand on the dining table that always had a homemade cake on display in the center. I sat down, put Bonnie in my lap, and stuck a few crumbs in her mouth. She giggled while she nibbled, showing four tiny teeth at the bottom and two at the top.

"You wanna give the baby some Kool-Aid?" she said, pouring a big glass full of Cherry, my favorite flavor. "I know you don't like to drink behind other people."

"Oh, no thank you," I said. "She can share mine."

Aunt Judy went into the kitchen and started washing dishes. Bonnie and I were enjoying the cake and Kool-

Aid when she surprised me and asked, "How would you feel if Blossom had another baby?"

I choked on my drink. "Mama ought to be shot if she has another baby! What made you ask that question?"

"No patickler reason," she said.

I stared at her, but her back was turned to me as she washed dishes.

"How do you like going to Madison High School?" she said. "Homer really like playing on the football team. I hope I get to see my son out on that field someday."

"I like it just fine," I said. I knew she was talking about how Uncle Clyde was always too busy going here and there to go watch his husky son play ball. I wished I could go see Homer, who was my age, play linebacker, but the games were all at night and the last city bus to the country leaves downtown at five o'clock. I felt sorry for her because they had a truck, but she was stuck at home most of the time.

"I wish I could join the school choir, but I don't have any way to get home if I stay after school to practice. So, I'll just have to settle for hearing the students sing." We both wish for something that might never happen, I thought.

A horn beeped. "Let's go!" Uncle Clyde hollered as he cranked up the truck.

I jumped up with Bonnie in my arms.

"I'll get that saucer," she said. "Thank ya'll both for coming to visit me."

"You're welcome. Tell Aunt Judy bye-bye," I said in baby talk as I waved Bonnie's hand and ran toward the door.

On the short ride back home, I bounced giggling Bonnie on my lap while thinking of Aunt Judy's question. How would I feel if Mama had another baby? My stomach churned like words were building up inside me, making me so full that they needed to burst forth. Mama would get angry, but I was determined to ask if another baby surprise was coming to our house.

Mama was in her bedroom sitting at the sewing machine when I burst into her room and laid Bonnie on the bed.

"Aunt Judy asked me how I'd feel about you having another baby. Are you going to have another baby?"

Without looking up or taking her foot off the pedal, she mumbled an answer. "Yeah, but you don't have to worry 'bout this one," she said. "Miss Johnson already asked if she could have it."

"Good!" I said. "And this time please tell us when you're not going to come home. We were worried the last time when you were gone three whole days and we didn't know what happened to you."

I turned and walked out of the room satisfied that at least I knew the truth and didn't have to wonder about it anymore.

***

About two months after my talk with Aunt Judy, Mama, now age forty-six, gave birth to Yvette, her eighteenth child. This time Drunk Mr. Fred dropped off Mama and her package—a tiny, chocolate baby that had no idea what life had in store for her. I turned my head when she came in the house carrying a pink receiving blanket.

For five days I tried my best to ignore Yvette when she cried. I didn't change her diaper or feed her Carnation formula. Poor thing, she sucked her bottle like she was starving to death. I hoped Mama noticed that there was another hungry mouth in our house. Every day I wondered when the baby giveaway would take place.

On the sixth day after Yvette's arrival, I came home from school and noticed there was no crying baby in the living room or bedroom. Mama was in the kitchen cooking.

"Where's Yvette?" I said. "Did you give her away like she was a cup of sugar?"

The thought of Mama giving away her baby had been bothering me ever since she told me her plan. The helpless baby needed somebody to speak for her. How could I stand by and say nothing. I would want somebody to fight for me. How could a mother not care about her own baby?

"What you talking 'bout?" Mama said. "I gave her to old Mr. and Mrs. Johnson like I told you. Now you can stop actin' like she ain't here."

"I acted ugly," I said. "Families need to stay together! You gave away Sulema and Vickie. Wasn't that enough?" My boldness surprised me. Words kept rolling off my tongue. The more we talked, the angrier I became.

Mama turned away from the stove and stared at me like I had gone crazy.

I glared at her from across the room. First I'd lost respect for Daddy, and now Mama. How could I let another of my sisters grow up not knowing her family and do nothing to help? Why would a woman have a baby if you didn't want it?

"Go take Yvette back!" I said, thinking, God must have put me in this family to fight for the children.

"I can't do that," Mama said.

"Then I will," I said.

Rushing out the door with Vera following close behind, I trotted along the path through the woods in front of our house on the other side of Cashmere Road, fussing all the way. I thought about my sisters Vickie and Sulema growing up without knowing us because Mama had given them away when they were babies. Not this time!

The Johnson's cows grazed inside a wooden fence as I ran past them and then up the steps to their front porch. I banged on the front door. Mrs. Johnson opened right away with a puzzled look on her face.

"I've come to take my baby sister back home," I said.

"Your Mama gave her to us," she said.

"Well, she changed her mind. She sent me to bring her back home now. She'll let you babysit her when she goes back to work."

Mrs. Johnson hesitated for a moment then left me standing on her front porch with the door open. In a few minutes, she returned carrying Yvette wrapped up in a pink blanket. She handed me the diaper bag and I passed it to Vera who stood behind me. Then, with trembling hands she clumsily placed the sleeping baby in my out-stretched arms.

"Thank you," I said. "Our family has to stay together." I was glad Vera had joined me so she could see that sometimes we have to fight for our little sisters and brother. She'll have to make these big decisions after I leave home, I thought.

Clutching my baby sister close to my bosom, I rushed back home as fast as my legs could carry me through the woods. I never looked back, but I heard the diaper bag on Vera's shoulder flapping in the wind.

"Mama ought to know that lady and her husband are too old to take care of a baby," I shouted. I heard an echo from the trees. They agreed.

I felt wonderful! I'd done a good deed and saved a baby's life. I'd succeeded in intercepting Mama's plans to become a child donor, again. "Thank you God!" I shouted. "We all belong together and that's just how it's going to be!"

"You've got courage!" Vera said. "I'm proud to be your little sister."

I thought about how confused fourteen-year-old Vickie had looked when I visited Orangeburg at twelve and told her that she was my big sister. Only God knows how Sulema's getting along with her old adopted parents in Marshall Village.

Yvette, Mama's eighteenth baby, looked like a cute doll with long wavy hair. By the time she was three months old, we began asking each other, "Who do you think her daddy is?" Then we all started asking each other, "Who's your daddy?"

Mama ignored the question whenever one of us asked, "Who's my daddy?" She just said, "You're here, ain't you? That's all that matters."

I remembered that one time my drunk Daddy told me, "You're mine. At least your mama say you is." Those words stung me like a needle breaking the skin. Wasn't being married to Mama and naming me after him enough proof that I was his daughter? I thought his liquor was talking, but later on I realized that he was serious. No wonder some people say, "Mama's baby, Daddy's maybe."

God, why didn't you fix it so a man can know when he's made a woman pregnant? Everybody can see a pregnant woman. Well, everybody except me when it's my own mama. But how do you recognize the baby's daddy?

I thought about the pregnant girls at Corinthian Baptist Church being forced to go stand in front of the congregation and say, "I have sinned." Not one time has any boy ever stood up and made a confession. The girl didn't get pregnant by herself. That is so unfair.

It hurt to hear my sisters and brother asking, "What's my daddy's name?" They didn't ask for their daddy, they just wanted to know his name. But they couldn't even get that. Since Mama never divulged the names of fathers, curiosity led us to make up a guessing game about which one of Mama's boyfriends might be each child's father.

"Mama and Daddy never filed for divorce," I told the younger ones. "That's why we all have Mama's last name. But I don't know that David Kincaid even knows about Mama's last four babies. I never mentioned them because he told me to mind my own business after I told him that she gave Sulema away." Does a woman have the right to do whatever she wants with her baby? What if her husband doesn't agree with her decision?

One day while the daddy guessing game was on, I said, "Rather than try to solve this unknown daddy mystery, let's thank God that we at least have a single mother who is willing to stay in a house with a bunch of noisy children. At least we know each other. What good is knowing who your daddy is if he's not doing anything for you? At least my daddy gives us food money every week."

"Sis, how do you know Daddy is your daddy?" Harry said.

"Because he's the only daddy I've ever known!" I said.

Harry's question bothered me. We needed to stop wasting time talking about what used to be, could be, should be, ought to be, or might be. "I'm appointing myself to be the one to make a difference in this family," I said. "I'm going to make good grades, graduate from high school, go away to college, get a good job, and help Mama move into a decent house."

"Sounds like you want to do a lot, Sis," Harry said. "We'll have to wait and see what you do for real. It would be good if you just do two of those things."

"Do you think Daddy will say, 'Davida's my daughter,' when I become successful?"

"I bet he will," Harry said.

"Yep. I'm going to make sure that the only daddy I know comes to my graduation so I can make him and Mama proud of me. You'll see."

Chapter 11
THE TRUTH
ABOUT DADDY

FOR ALMOST TWO YEARS, I shopped every Saturday at Hamilton's Grocery Store whether I saw Daddy or not. I liked bagging groceries and helping Amanda stock supplies. The work was fun, quite different from changing baby diapers and doing housework. Tips from customers who gave me their extra change made me want to work harder to please them.

Mr. Hamilton and Amanda drove me all the way home with my groceries. I bought everything we needed from his store, including extra things I wanted like costume jewelry and stockings to wear to church on Sunday. Amanda talked to me about girl issues like makeup, hairstyles and hygiene. She was the perfect big sister to me.

One day I entered the store and Amanda greeted me saying, "My daddy wants to see you in his office right away."

"Okay," I said. I rushed toward the back of the store expecting to receive the offer of a part-time job as a bag girl at fifteen. After tapping on the window, I waited for the usual, "C'mon in." Instead, he took off his glasses, got out of his swivel chair, and then came and stood in the doorway.

"Davida," he whispered, "I hate to say this, but I had to close your daddy's account. We haven't seen him in three whole weeks." He sounded like he had a frog in his throat that was choking off his words.

"Ohhh, I didn't know that." I stared at him wondering what I should say or do or think. Did he think that I knew the bill had not been paid? I was ashamed that Daddy had not kept his promise. I felt stupid for expecting to be offered a job, but glad I hadn't shared that thought with Amanda. Had I come all the way across town for nothing? How could I return home empty-handed? After what seemed like a long time, I said, "Thank you, sir, for letting me shop the last two weeks. I really didn't know Daddy hadn't paid his bill. I'll go see if I can find him."

"I'm very sorry," he said. "But I need my customers to pay every week."

"I'm sorry, too." I headed for the door before the teardrops fell. Amanda said, "Goodbye," as I rushed toward the door, but I was too embarrassed to look at her. How could Daddy disappoint such nice people? Suddenly, I wondered if something bad had happened to him. I felt guilty for failing to check on him when I knew he had no family in Columbia except us. Did I care more about his money than about him? My stomach churned like it was afraid of everything bad that could have happened.

I hurried to Daddy's rented room beneath the old woman's house and knocked loud enough to wake a sleeping drunk. No answer. Convinced that he wasn't at home, I walked across town and found him half drunk at one of his three liquor houses near the City Shed. Thank goodness his favorite place to get drunk with his buddy, Mr. Joe, had not changed.

"Daddy, Deacon Hamilton said you haven't been in the store to pay your grocery bill in three weeks. Why didn't you tell me?"

"Shucks, I forgot all 'bout that account when I moved closer to my job," he said, laughing. He leaned back in the chair and swished his head as if to douse his brain with liquor.

"You moved!" Aw shucks! Why did he have to mess up a good thing? I dreaded the thought of having to beg for money again and take food home on the bus.

"Wanna see where I live now?" Before I could answer, he pulled himself up and staggered toward the door, saying, "See ya'll later alligators."

As I followed Daddy out the door, Mr. Joe, with slurred speech, hollered, "After while crocodile." Their favorite saying and the response had not changed, either.

For two blocks he had room on the sidewalk to sway to the right and left before turning into the driveway of a big red brick house. At a side door, he hobbled up three steps and went inside a screened-in porch.

"Hey David! Who dat wid ya?" yelled a slobber-mouth drunk walking down a long hallway with closed doors on both sides. Locks clicked, doors opened and heads poked out.

Nosy men! I stepped closer to my daddy, wanting to hurry out of there.

The man came closer and stopped, tilted his head to one side and eyed me like I was a hunk of meat to be inspected. He acted like he needed a pair of eyeglasses.

"Dis my daughter, ya'll," Daddy said. We walked down the hall and he introduced me to three ex-husbands and two ex-wives, occupants of the rented rooms. They all smelled like alcohol and had little or no furniture in their rooms.

"Hi," was all I said. I smiled as I listened to them talk about the children they hadn't seen in a long time, but I really wanted to get out of that house of sorrows.

As we were leaving, Daddy entered a bathroom next to the communal kitchen. I leaned against the bathroom door until he pushed it. Then I ran outside, threw up both arms, and took a deep breath. It felt good to be back in the beautiful sunshine and fresh air. How depressing to see a house full of used-to-be-parents-turned-drunks!

At the end of the driveway, Daddy stopped in front of what looked like a detached garage covered with red bricks. I was proud of him for choosing to move above ground.

When I stepped through the door behind him, the smell of old urine hit my nostrils like it had been squirted into my face. I gasped and ran to open a window. That's when I noticed a night pot like the one we used in the country that probably hadn't been emptied in weeks. The room had a double bed, a dinette table with rusty legs, a lamp, a kerosene heater, a chair, and a rope hanging wall-to-wall for a closet.

Daddy had to go inside the big house to bathe, shave, cook, and use the bathroom because his new room had no sink and no water. His city house was almost as bad as ours out in the country. He was having a rough time for someone who worked six days a week and had no children at home. How could he live like this?

The odor must have hit him too, because he took the night pot out to empty it.

I stood against an open screen door to allow air to enter while I tried to decide which room I disliked the most, Daddy's old slave quarters or the converted garage. Neither was good for humans, but it was nice to see him stand up straight and walk through his front door without bending over like a slave. He deserved better than that. In his new place he could get fresh air through a window or the door. And the best part was that I wouldn't have to walk far to reach the city bus line.

A person's lifestyle sure can change after the family falls apart, I thought, when I saw Daddy coming back, swinging the night pot by the handle. He handed me five dollars, and I took off, eager to go home and tell Mama what happened.

All Mama said was, "Nothing you tell me 'bout David will surprise me."

The next Saturday I met Daddy at noon when he knocked off work. He didn't give me food money right away so I followed him home. This time his front door was already open when we got there. I was shocked to see Aunt Judy's best friend, pop-eyed Miss Annie Mae, sitting on the side of my daddy's bed.

"Hey there!" Daddy said. He sounded like he knew she was there all along.

"You're home!" she said, smiling to show off her gold tooth. She sat with her legs crossed at the knee, shaking one foot like she was nervous. A folded Ebony magazine was in her hand.

Why was she acting like she was at home? Had she spent the night in my daddy's room? Then I remembered hearing Mama say, "David's going with my sister-in-law's best friend." My eyes scanned the room, especially the makeshift clothes rack, for evidence that Miss Annie lived with him. I didn't see any women's clothes.

"Annie, ya know Davida?" Daddy said.

"Yeah. I know all your children. Hey Davida."

"Hi," I said, even though I didn't want to be polite. I recognized her from all the times she came to Uncle Clyde's house when we lived in Marshall Village. I felt so uncomfortable. Daddy should be with Mama, not her. If he had known she was there, he should have warned me.

I guess she sensed my discomfort because she looked down at the magazine and started reading. I looked around the small room and then walked over to one window and looked outside. The view was of a dead tree trunk beside a chain-linked fence. When I turned around, I noticed that Daddy was gone.

"Where did Daddy go?" I said.

"He went to the house to get some ice. He'll be back in a minute. Go on and sit over in that chair."

"Thank you." I sat in the only padded dinette chair at the table and wondered where the other chair was. It seemed so awkward hearing another woman tell me to sit down in my daddy's room.

We both waited in silence. I stared at an old newspaper on the table until I heard Daddy whistling as he approached the room. Again I recognized Ray Charles' song and began singing along with him, "I've got a woman, way cross town, and she's good to me." He whistled that song whenever he was in a good mood.

He brought in a small bucket of ice and two glasses that he handed to his pop-eyed girlfriend. It seemed like he'd forgotten I was there until he turned toward me.

"Davida, I got something for you, too." He reached in his

pocket and pulled out a ten-dollar bill and handed it to me. "Here," he said, grinning.

"Gee, thanks Daddy!" I said. He wasn't drunk yet and I didn't have to beg. What a new attitude! I accepted the money and gave him a big hug.

Miss Annie Mae stared at the floor and smiled.

"I guess I'll be going now. I'll see you next week." I waved and darted out the door before he could reply. I heard them laughing as I left. Their plan to get rid of me worked. Ten dollars couldn't buy much food anymore, but it was better than nothing.

Mama had told the truth about Daddy and Miss Annie Mae – she was the woman Daddy had gone to live with when our family broke up. Even though it bothered me to see her sitting on his bed, I congratulated myself for pretending not to be surprised. I skipped along the sidewalk saying, "Self, I am so proud of you! You handled that situation very well. Thank you Miss Annie Mae. That's the quickest I've ever gotten money from my daddy. You can be there every Saturday."

Too bad Miss Annie Mae wasn't there the next time I visited Daddy's room.

Chapter 12

DISGUSTED DAUGHTER

STANDING AT THE BUS STOP in the July sun, I felt like a parched peanut in the shell.

"I think I'm gonna pass out in this heat if the bus don't hurrup," a stout woman said. She held a white parasol over her head, but perspiration rolled down into her bosom and formed a crescent moon across the front of her sleeveless yellow blouse.

"At last! Hours late but here it comes." I said, as the bus came into view.

Dying of thirst, I wiped my forehead with the back of my hand as the woman climbed onboard in slow motion. Catching the early morning bus again reminded me of how much I dreaded begging Daddy for money.

My daddy had already left work when I arrived. All the way to his house I kept wishing he had not moved from his room near Hamilton's Grocery Store. He wasn't there either. So, in the sweltering heat, I walked toward Henley Homes wondering what shape perspiration would form across my breasts. My red pedal pushers and candy-striped tank top stuck to my skin like Elmer's glue to paper. Sweat trickled down my back.

Swinging my index finger, I said, "Eeny meeny miny mo, tell me where I need to go." I pointed to building 14-C, the closest liquor house to Daddy's job. I stood on the stoop and knocked. Amid talking and laughter on the other side of the screen door, Brook Benton co-oed to Dinah Washington, "Baby, You've Got What It Takes." I waited a few minutes, then knocked again, louder this time.

Watching Daddy and his drinking buddies get intoxicated was disgusting. I hated all the times that I had no choice but to tag along and wait until he paid his liquor bill and took his first drink. That's when he decided how much to give me. I stuck close to him like a shadow, so no dirty old man would grope me. I also reminded him to get his change before one of those whorish waitresses stuffed it in her bra.

Foul-smelling old men and women with rotten teeth and bad breath were always present in the liquor houses. The last time I tagged along with Daddy, a skinny old woman wearing a short skirt and low-cut top, saw him and hollered, "Here's my hero!" She ran over to him like he was some kind of celebrity. I knew she wanted money just like I did.

Someone fumbled with the latch and interrupted my thoughts. The woman who liked to say, "David is my hero," unlatched the screen door.

"Is my Daddy here?" I said, thinking, I bet she saw me standing at the door long before she opened it.

"Yeah, my hero's in here," she said. As I stepped into the room, she yelled, "Look who's here, David!"

Daddy glanced over at me, turned his shot glass up to his lips, and emptied it. He slammed the glass down on the table and licked his lips. I approached an empty seat at his little round table.

"Davida knows how to find me," he flubbed.

I feigned a smile as I walked across the smoke-filled room. The smell of liquor filled the air.

Women served drinks on a little tray, switching their hips as they walked a few steps from the kitchen to the living room. They leaned all over the men and stroked their chests after they put drinks on the table. Daddy and the other men slapped them on their buttocks or slid their hands down their thighs, and then laughed when the waitresses cried, "Ouch!"

Dirty jokes were exchanged as usual until one man looked at me and said, "Ya'll watch your mouth! David's daughter's here."

Couldn't Daddy see they love his money more than him? They knew he would spend all his pay and then start drinking on credit.

"All drinks on me!" a juicy-mouthed man slobbered.

"Next round's on me," said another.

Daddy chimed in with a broad grin, "I'll wait my turn." He talked like a big spender. I knew that his fat bankroll was loaded with one-dollar bills that would soon disappear unless I stopped him.

The men acted like the drinks were free, but I watched as the housekeeper added the costs to their tabs as quickly as they yelled: "Gin and tonic, Scotch on the rocks, Vodka and orange juice, Rum and Coke...." Some drinks cost more than others but only the housekeeper saw the tab. Anybody with common sense would know they were being cheated.

Everyone in the liquor house was repulsive to me, including my own daddy. But since the account at Hamilton's Grocery Store was closed, I had no choice but to try to get the ten dollars we needed. Hungry mouths at home forced me to make the weekly Saturday morning trip.

"Daddy," I whispered, "let's go to your house. All this cigarette smoke is bothering me and it's too hot to be sitting in here." I spoke directly to him, but a hush fell over the room. I knew they wanted to hear his response. He usually told me to wait awhile, but this time he didn't.

"All right, Davida. Let's go." He grabbed my arm and I led the way as he staggered out of there. He didn't drink liquor before he left Mama. If he was happy with Miss Annie Mae, then why was he drinking so much? Was he trying to be like Drunk Mr. Fred, Mama's old boyfriend?

Daddy never asked me anything about Mama or our family. So, I said, "Did you forget about all your children just because we don't live in the same house with you?"

He mumbled something, but it wasn't the answer to my question.

"What's my name, Daddy?" I said. I thought he'd give a quick answer because he named me Davida after him.

He mumbled some gibberish.

"How could a father not miss his own children?" I said.

He didn't answer.

"It's not fair that Mama should have to take care of all the children by herself and you spend more money on liquor in one day than we spend on food for a whole week!" I shouted.

Again, he said nothing.

We continued the slow walk home in silence until I said, "Give me your key."

He reached in his pocket, pulled out a key, and mumbled, "Hmmm."

Was he pretending not to hear what I said?

He leaned against the brick wall and handed me the key. I unlocked the door and then pulled him inside until he reached the bed that looked like it hadn't been made up all week. He plopped down and fell backwards with his feet on the floor. I removed his dirty brogan boots and pulled his stinky feet up on the bed. While I propped a pillow beneath his head, Daddy reached in his pocket and pulled out a ten-dollar-bill.

"Here. I'm giving you this 'cause you mine," he said. "At least your mama say ya mine."

"Don't say that to me! That's a strange thing for a father to say to his own child. Those words hurt."

For a moment I stared at the drunk lying on his back with his eyes closed. He should have been thanking me for rescuing him from those vultures rather than saying something stupid. I thought of a few nasty things I could say about him but kept quiet.

When I took the money out of his hand, Daddy grabbed my arm and yanked me. I fell on top of him and struggled to keep from sinking in the middle of the soft mattress.

"What are you doing?" I cried.

His grip was tight. I couldn't pull away, so I bit his hand and he let go of my arm. Clutching the cash, I scrambled off the bed and ran out of there without looking back.

On the bus ride home, I kept my face toward the window so no one would notice my tears. I rehearsed how I would tell Mama that I was not going to meet Daddy again. On the three-mile walk home from the bus stop, I kept wondering how my own Daddy could treat me like I was one of those women in the liquor houses. Did he forget who I was? Was that his way of getting rid of me? Did the spirits of alcohol trick him into thinking I was Miss Annie Mae in his room? Why had God allowed that to happen to me?

At home, I stared into Mama's eyes as I handed her the money.

"I am never going to meet Daddy again! So, please don't ask me. And I will never ever drink alcohol in my life!"

Mama stared back at me without saying a word. I knew she understood that it was time for a change. And I was taking the first step. How were we going to make it without Daddy's money?

We'll be okay, I thought. In six months, I can get a job after I turn sixteen. I just don't know what to do until then.

Chapter 13
GOOD CREDIT

LESS MONEY MEANT LESS FOOD at home. Since I created the shortage by not going to meet Daddy anymore, I followed his example and opened an account at Marvin's Grocery Store, a mile from our house. With no money to pay the bill, I saved my $2.00 credit limit for an emergency.

One Thursday, I tried hard to stretch a dinner of stewed tomatoes and rice. But after feeding everyone else there wasn't enough for me to get any. So I took my twelve-year-old sister Vera along for company to the store owned by my classmate Rosa Lee's father.

"You'll have to be in charge at home when I get my first job," I said. Vera and I talked about Mama needing help to feed all the children.

"Well, I'm in no hurry to do all you do," she said. "It was pretty clever of you to open an account at the store and you don't even have a job."

"We do what we can and pray about everything else," I said. "Rosa Lee talked to her daddy for me because she knew I wouldn't have asked for help unless I needed it. We get some things in this world based on who we know rather than what we have."

The country store, which was built with slabs of lumber and a tin roof, was closed when we arrived. I went to the brick house next door and tapped on Rosa Lee's front bedroom window. She pulled aside the sheer white curtains and peered into the dark.

"Who is it?" she said.

"It's me, Davida. I need to buy some food."

"Just a minute." The curtain fell back in place as she turned and walked away.

Vera and I went to wait in front of the store.

Tall Rosa Lee came outside carrying a bunch of keys on a big metal ring. She fumbled with the lock several times before finding the right key. Inside, she flicked the light switch and dingy, fluorescent bulbs revealed the dusty room. Rows of empty metal shelves were everywhere. Near the door was a wide glass counter with a cash register on one end. The place looked like a ghost town. The only thing missing was tumbleweed.

Rosa Lee stepped behind the counter.

"What would you like to buy?" she said.

She became a different person when she stood behind the counter. I liked her business lady voice. She sounded like a telephone operator who knew the answer to every question.

"Let me see what you've got," I said.

Vera stood on one end of the glass counter drawing in the thick dust on top with her index finger while I walked along the empty counters eyeing the merchandise. Chicken feed, mouse traps, Raid for roaches, lime for snakes...

"Um, do you have any cookies?" I asked, knowing that her family would have already eaten all the good food they stocked.

"No, we doesn't have any," she said.

"What about Raisin Bran?"

"We doesn't carry that."

"It's bad business having a store that doesn't stock items people want to buy," I said. "I'll bet you lose a lot of customers." I was certain she knew that, but I just couldn't resist telling her anyway. I was also showing Vera how customers behaved at Hamilton's Grocery Store.

"If you don't see it, then we doesn't have it," she said, staring at me.

Behind her, in the middle of the bottom wall shelf, were two large boxes of Saltine crackers, tall cans of Pork-n-Beans, flat cans of sardines, little round cans of Potted Meat and Vienna Sausages, and one odd-shaped can of Spam. At least I had some food to choose from to make my walk and her opening the store worthwhile.

"I'll have a can of mustard sardines and a box of Saltines, I said, pointing.

"Oh." Turning around like she didn't know the food was there, Rosa Lee removed the two items and dropped them in a brown paper sack. Only three cans of sardines were left. Time to reorder, I thought, wondering if she knew that.

In an adding machine beside the cash register, she punched in fifteen cents plus ten cents. Surely she knew that was twenty-five cents, I thought, scratching my head. Couldn't her brain add those two numbers?

"That will be twenty-five cents," she said.

"Put it on my account. I'll pay you later."

"Okay." She used a pencil to write the correct amount in a brown receipt register. It was the same Standard General Ledger that Amanda had at Hamilton's grocery store.

"Thank you," I said, taking my bag. Vera went outside ahead of me and we waited until Rosa Lee turned off the lights and locked the door. I didn't want to leave her alone in grocery ghost town.

"It sure would be nice to have a real store out here," Vera said as we headed home. "Those little cans of meat looked cute. But our family would need to buy everything on that shelf and a whole lot more."

We both laughed.

"Well, at least we know they *does* carry good ole Pork'n'Beans," Vera said, mimicking Rosa Lee. That's a change from our usual black-eyed peas, lima beans, butter beans, great northern beans, navy beans, kidney beans and my favorite, pinto beans. Gee, you know, that's a different bean for every day of the week. I'd have a problem deciding when to eat Pork'n'Beans."

"Real-life situations can teach you creative ways to solve math problems in school," I said. "You've got a problem deciding which day of the week to eat Pork 'n'Beans. My problem is how to pay for them. I didn't have any money, but I found a way to get food. I didn't have anything to eat, but now I do and I don't have to cook it. This whole world is a classroom where hands-on instruction enables you to respond to various situations in interesting, memorable, and fun ways."

"That sounds good! I just don't understand what it means," she giggled.

"I like talking to you," I said. "Too bad you can't solve my credit problem."

When we got home, I hid the food beneath my sweater so nobody would ask me to share. Vera kept the little ones away from the kitchen while I ate my sardines from the can and one of the four packs of Saltines in the box.

While at the table, I scribbled a problem on back of the brown paper bag and solved it just for fun. I multiplied to find out how much I would save if I bought a $3.59 canned ham on sale for twenty percent off. I multiplied by .20 and rounded the solution to $.72. Some students would have had a hard time with that problem. But I didn't. I stared at my answer and thought, Now I need to figure out how to pay my grocery bill for real.

My love for math might make me rich one day. And I'd never be hungry again.

I woke up Friday morning thinking of Rosa Lee and the bill I needed to pay. I need money now, and I can't wait until I turn sixteen to get a job, I thought.

After finding the address of the employment office in the phone book and leaving Vera in charge, I went downtown to get a job. I saw my reflection as I walked past a glass wall before entering the double doors of a brick building on Sumter Street. I admired my skinny profile in a navy blue skirt, striped sleeveless blouse and penny loafers, minus the coins.

"You look cute, Miss Almost Sixteen," I mumbled. "I'd hire you."

Inside, I strolled over to the receptionist's desk, wondering what to say.

"I'm here to apply for a job," I said.

"Sign in and take a seat over there," the woman said. "Fill out the application."

I listened to her, thinking, "Why does she have a southern drawl and I don't? Why do people who live in the same town talk differently?" I went over and sat on a bench in the Colored section and worked on my application. Across the room was the White Only waiting area. In the large room were several men and women, mostly Negroes. I noticed that I was the youngest person there. I didn't care.

An elderly woman with round black–rimmed glasses with lenses too big for her face called, "Davida Kincaid." I mimicked her accent as I painted a smile on my face and strolled over to her desk. Her nameplate read Miss White. "Yep, that's her," I thought.

"Are you aware that you have to be sixteen before we can send you out on a job interview?" she said.

"Yes ma'am. I am." She could interpret "I am" however she chose.

Miss White handed me an application that asked a hundred questions including my name, address, date of birth, date available for work, and reason for seeking employment. For the last question I wrote, "My family needs food money today." That was a great reason to get a job. She eyeballed the document and then turned it over for me to sign. Without reading the typed paragraph above, I signed on the dotted line at the bottom. Putting my application in a pile, she looked into my eyes for the first time and said, "Just a minute."

Miss White shuffled a pile of papers on her desk until she found the one she wanted. Holding the receiver to her ear, she used a fountain pen to dial a number. "I have a young lady in my office who's available to work today," she said. She listened for a moment and then said, "I'll send her over."

"Keeble's Café needs a dishwasher right away," she said, hanging up. "They'll pay you in cash today – one dollar an hour."

"I'll take it," I said. Getting paid in cash on the same day was better than I had imagined.

Miss White's pen moved in slow motion as she wrote the address in excellent penmanship. I wanted to scream, "Hurry up!"

"Give this letter to Mr. Maddox. He's expecting you." She placed the letter in an envelope, licked the flap, and sealed it.

"Thank you," I said, being careful not to snatch the letter before I rushed out of the building. Skipping over to Keeble's cafe near the University of South Carolina's campus, I figured I could work from eleven until four o'clock and earn $5.00 before catching the last bus to the country. Five minutes later, moments before the Big Ben downtown struck eleven times, I knocked on the kitchen door.

I thought about canned biscuits when the door opened and a fluffy-looking white cook with a sweaty brow popped in front of me and reached for the letter. He was dressed in all white – including his chef's hat and the dingy apron that seemed to be choking his fat neck.

"They phoned to say you'd be here soon," he said, panting like he might give out of breath any moment. He stuffed the letter in his apron pocket like it was a piece of trash. "C'mon in. The regular boy didn't come in today. We already got a sink full o dishes and a dining room full o' customers."

Butch, according to his nametag, pointed to the double-sided stainless steel sink attached to the wall next to the kitchen door. Both basins, long as my arms, were full of soapy water and dirty dishes.

In his thick southern accent Butch said, "Just fetch one a dem aprons and go to work. Gal, lotsa hungry folk need ya rat now." He pointed to a row of aprons hanging from a wire hook on the wall next to a swinging door. While I got the apron, Butch disappeared behind some huge white stoves on the other side of the kitchen.

"I'll show him I can work just as well as any sixteen year old," I mumbled. Happy that I'd worn a sleeveless blouse, I immersed my arms in the sink and began washing and rinsing plates, saucers, cups, bowls, glasses and silverware. I worked non-stop from eleven until almost one o'clock. I could hear the noisy lunch crowd, but all I could see were soapsuds and armfuls of dirty dishes that busboys brought through the swinging doors. Every time I almost finished a stack of dishes, a busboy showed up and dumped another one in the sink.

When there was less chatter in the dining room and no deliveries for a long time, I wondered if I could work until four if all the customers were gone by one o'clock. Maybe I worked myself out of a job, I thought, pulling my arms out of the water.

I had no idea my skin could absorb water like a sponge until I noticed that my arms and hands were swollen and wrinkled like prunes. The sunken and puffy sections of my arm went all the way to my biceps. I rubbed them dry, but wondered how long before they would return to normal. "Lord, please let this be a temporary condition," I muttered.

A blond-haired busboy burst through the swinging doors with an armful of plates and blurted, "The crunch is over!" He dropped his load in the sink and it made a loud splash. He slapped his hands together like his job was finished and returned to the dining room.

Speechless, I stared at the large pile of dishes in the sink. I groaned. I'd been so busy busting suds that I'd forgotten about the people in the restaurant.

All I could think about was my puffy arms, and the time years ago when a skinny deaf mute jumped into the Broad River to save a drowning boy. They both drowned. His body looked ten times bigger when he was pulled from the water and stuffed in a black bag. I always wondered if the swelling ever went down. No job was worth killing my arms.

Maybe the regular dishwasher quit before his arms rotted off!

Without saying a word, I yanked off the apron, tossed it on a hook, and then dashed out the back door.

"That's it. I quit!" I said, feeling like a freed slave. "They are not going to work me to death for a lousy two dollars. Next time, I'll get a real job and get paid."

Chapter 14
A REAL JOB

WE NEEDED MORE FOOD THAN ever during the summer vacation. With hungry mouths expecting to be fed every day for breakfast and dinner, I realized how much the free lunch program helped families like ours during the school year.

My Daddy hadn't paid his food bill, but I wanted to pay mine. Rosa Lee trusted me with credit and I didn't want to disappoint her. So when I reached my two-dollar limit at Marvin's Grocery Store, I went back to the employment office even though my dishwasher experience had made me job-shy.

I prayed as I filled out a new application, God, please let a different clerk call me this time? PLEASE? I don't want to have to explain to Miss White why I quit that dishwasher job. I didn't really lie about being the minimum age. Fifteen and a half rounds to sixteen.

You know Mama was denied welfare because she pays no rent to live in the house her brother built on their property. Who made that rule? Don't they know people can't eat land? She was so disappointed that day when she brought home two foods that made us constipated, a five-pound box of government cheese and a big silver can of dry peanut butter with oil swimming on the top.

"We's be too 'po' to afford the 'o-r' on the end of "poor," I was thinking, when a woman called my name.

"Davida Kincaid."

I headed toward the desk of Mrs. Jefferson, according to her nameplate. She was a red-haired lady with freckles. Good. I'd talk to someone other than Miss White. My heart thumped a warning like the theme song to Dragnet when I saw her reading my application from two weeks ago.

She looked up at me and said with her southern drawl, "Have a seat. I think we got something here." She turned the paper in her hand around and pointed to a babysitting job in Myrtle Beach, South Carolina. "It's an opportunity to vacation while watching a family's small children. You can have fun on the beach and earn twenty dollars for six days work. Transportation and meals are included."

"I'll take it," I said. I had plenty of experience babysitting. Traveling out of Columbia sounded like an adventure. A trip to the beach with all expenses paid. Wow!

Mrs. Jefferson called the O'Leary family and made all the arrangements. She placed the employment letter in an envelope, licked the flap and sealed it. Before handing me the letter, she scribbled a note containing the family's address, phone number, and the date and time they planned to leave on Sunday.

Riding home on the bus, I pictured myself walking on the beach like I'd done at Coney Island when I was fourteen. I envisioned a boardwalk, music, juicy hotdogs, and huge waves thrashing the shoreline in the evening. The ride to Cashmere Road seemed much shorter that day and so was the walk home. I rushed into the house and shouted my good news.

"Mama, I'm going to Myrtle Beach for six days. The O'Leary family promised to pay me twenty dollars for babysitting their three small children."

"Don't you hafta be sixteen to get a job," she said.

"Well, I'm almost sixteen."

"I hope them people don't trick ya," Mama said. "You can't quit that job."

"They won't. This time, I'm going to get my pay."

On Sunday, I caught the bus to the O'Leary house near the Carolina Coliseum. When I arrived, the family was packing the back of a station wagon that had a wood trim along the doors. Mrs. O'Leary, with long brown hair hanging over her shoulders looked pretty in her red shorts and white t-shirt.

"Hi. Mrs. O'Leary, I said, handing her the letter. "I'm Davida from the employment office."

"Welcome," she said in that familiar southern drawl. "Give my husband your suitcase and then I'll introduce you to our boys." Mr. O'Leary, wearing shorts, a t-shirt, and a Gamecock baseball cap, grabbed my bag and stuffed it in the back.

Three boys raced out of the backyard toward the car. They finished in the order of their ages. She placed her hand on each one's head as they arrived. "Tim here, with the missing front tooth is five. Bobby here is three, and Adam's two. Ya'll say hey to Davida."

"Hey, Davida," they said in unison, staring at me like I was a chocolate tree. I wondered what they were thinking.

"Hey Tim, Bobby, and Adam," I said, looking into their blue eyes. Wearing only shorts and thongs (flip-flops), they were already dressed to play in the sand. Mama had said, "Look presentable for work," so I wore a skirt and sleeveless blouse. I'd packed a pair of thongs so I wouldn't have to walk barefoot in the sand, but I wished I had brought shorts just in case.

Mr. O'Leary grunted, "Okay" when Tim and Bobby claimed a window seat in the car. So, in the station wagon loaded with stuff, I sat in the middle of the backseat beside Adam wondering what new things I would see and do. The older boys rolled the windows up and down like they were winding up toys. Then they slumped over in the seat, sound asleep. I stared at the windshield as Mr. O'Leary drove to a part of South Carolina I had never seen before. I'd seen the movie Muscle Beach Party, starring Frankie Avalon and Annette Funicello, so I expected to have lots of fun and get paid.

When I carried my suitcase into the beach cabin after the two-hour ride, Mrs. O'Leary called me into the kitchen.

"Put that bag down and let me talk to you for a minute," she said. "We've got fam'ly members joining us. Always wait 'til we finish eatin' before you come in here. Then you can eat the leftovers before you clean up the kitchen. Do you understand me?"

"Yes ma'am," I said. Dang! Mama was right when she said that white woman would trick me. She seemed so nice but Mama knew she'd turn into a wicked stepmother and treat me like I was Cinderella. Did Mrs. Jefferson send me on this job to punish me for walking away from Keeble's Café?

"Now take the boys outside while we get settled."

After an hour of worrying that the three busy mice that I couldn't catch might run into the Atlantic Ocean and get swept away in their sky blue trunks, Mr. and Mrs. O'Leary came outside. He wore sky blue Speedos and she had on a royal blue bikini. This family gives me the blues, I thought.

Following them to the beach, I was surprised to see the boys walk between both parents like they were well behaved. I stood, waiting for instructions, while Mrs. O'Leary spread a blue and white striped beach towel on the sand.

"Let my boys play in the waves that wash ashore but don't let them go out in the water, you hear?" she said.

"Yes ma'am," I said.

"Boys, ya'll betta listen to Davida, ya hear? Don't go out in that water. Let the waves come to you. Ya'll hear me?

"Yes ma'am," they said. All three dashed toward the edge of the ocean before the words dripped from their lips. I was glad they all ran in the same direction.

Keeping them safe was a challenge. All afternoon the O'Leary couple sunbathed while I chased three hardheaded little boys all along the beach. With the adults glued to one spot, the boys ran wild. I could keep up with Adam, but Tim and Bobby ran around like startled chickens in a henhouse.

One time I saw their parents sit up and smear Coppertone on each other's backs and then turn over on their stomachs. I wondered how I was supposed to keep a low profile when I stood out from everybody on the crowded beach, except the other black nannies. Mr. and Mrs. O'Leary and all the other white folks lay baking in the sun all afternoon. Why didn't they stretch out in their own backyard to get a tan? Does it make sense to drive all the way to the beach and not get in the water? How could people who like a tanned complexion discriminate against people who have a natural tan?

I was exhausted by the time the toasted family went inside to eat dinner. Crouching outside by the kitchen door, I stared at the waves, longing to be free like them to go wherever, whenever I wanted. A tear wet my cheek. I wiped it away with my fist.

If Daddy had stayed with his family like Mr. O'Leary, then I wouldn't have to be out here, I thought.

Shivering and hungry by the time the kitchen was quiet, I went inside and saw ham slices, light bread, mustard, a bowl of potato chips, and sliced dill pickles. A cold sandwich wasn't the Sunday dinner I'd expected, but I stood at the counter and ate it as I eavesdropped on the hum of male and female southern voices in the living room and the loud television.

Mrs. Jefferson had not told me I'd have to eat leftovers. I felt like a mouse caught in a trap before it got a chance to nibble the cheese. I could do nothing but follow instructions until they took me back to Columbia on Friday. That first night I cleaned up the kitchen behind Mrs. O'Leary's parents, her grandparents, her sister and brother-in-law. Cleanup duty had not been listed on the job description I'd signed at the employment office.

Receiving little to eat after a whole day of hard work on Monday, I felt like Mrs. O'Leary hired a black person so she could mistreat me. So I became determined not to let her see me cry. She didn't know I had plenty of practice in going without food. She must not have heard that slaves ate *chitlins* and pig feet, not table scraps.

On Tuesday afternoon, Mrs. O'Leary's sister prepared

a crystal punch bowl full of homemade pimento cheese and covered it with Saran Wrap. The delicious-looking dish in the center of the table cried, "Eat me! Eat me." There was enough for everybody to have plenty and still have some left.

At dinnertime I sat outside doodling in the sand while the eleven family members in the kitchen raved about the food. They talked and talked. The chatter stopped when they left. Then I rushed inside to taste unsliced pimento cheese for the first time. I froze like a Popsicle when all I saw was an empty bowl with smear finger marks inside. They'd eaten every drop the same way I'd scraped cake batter off Mama's mixing bowl many times before. The only thing left was a colorful arrangement of rabbit food: raw carrots, broccoli, cucumbers, and celery. I didn't like any of that stuff. I started to cry but caught myself. I was too angry to risk letting any of those people see my tears. They ate more than vegetables. What made them think that's all I needed? "They're probably laughing at me now," I mumbled while washing the dishes. "God, I want to go home."

I finished cleaning the kitchen and then went to my bed, a quilt pallet on the floor.

Wednesday night while everyone was watching television, Tim, the oldest of the boys, looked over in the corner where I was sitting on my bed. He pointed his finger at me and hollered, "Davida, You lied! You ain't sixteen—." Before he could say another word, Mrs. O'Leary slapped her hand over his mouth.

I looked down at the patches in the quilt under me and pretended not to hear him. The grown ups had to be talking about me for Tim to say that. How did they find out? I wrestled with the thought of not getting paid again for all my hard work. Then I thought, "I'm going to get my twenty dollars!"

By Thursday I knew I could handle being treated like a slave because Friday was coming. That day passed quickly in spite of chasing the boys and cleaning up behind other people. I just couldn't decide which was worse, eating the table scraps or having to stay outdoors like a dog to wait for them.

At three o'clock on Friday afternoon I was tempted to shout "Hallelujah!" when we loaded the car and drove away from the cabin. I felt like a freed slave after President Abraham Lincoln signed the Emancipation Proclamation. I's going home now where I's belong, I thought, and the sooner I's be free from missa O'Leary, da betta.

I was startled when Mrs. O'Leary asked, "Davida, was this your first trip to the beach?"

"No ma'am. I went to the beach in New York."

"New York! You've been all the way to New York? When did you go there?"

"Last summer." I felt proud to say I'd gone somewhere other than Folly Beach, the only one in South Carolina where black folks could go to have fun.

"Did your family go on vacation?"

"Just me," I said. I could feel myself getting annoyed. God make her stop asking me questions! I wanted to holler as I sat behind her with my face turned to the station wagon window. It was peaceful in the back with her three sleeping boys slumped in the seat. Why couldn't they have been quiet like that just one day?

"Look at that long line of cars over there," Mr. O'Leary said. The two of them started talking about traffic headed toward the beach, and I got a chance to relax.

Two hours later we approached the State Capitol downtown. I'd missed the last bus to the country. I was trying to figure out how to get home when Mrs. O'Leary looked back at me.

"Would you like us to take you home?" she said. "My husband won't mind."

"Oh! Yes ma'am. But I live a long way out Main Street." I was too tired to care if they saw our blockhouse. I knew I'd never see them again, anyway.

"My wife is right," Mr. O'Leary said. "I like driving

along country roads and admiring the different trees. With the boys sleeping, the ride will be even better."

"Then go straight out Main Straight. I'll tell you where to turn."

I leaned back against the padded seat to enjoy the ride and dozed off a few times. Then I sat up when I felt the car go round the bend near my house.

"Davida, I knew you weren't sixteen yet, but I hired you anyway," Mrs. O'Leary said. "I figured you needed the money. Here's your pay." She held a twenty-dollar bill over the seat and I took it.

"Turn into that driveway," I said, glad that no children were in sight. I planned to hop out and go. Nobody would ever know how I got home.

Our front door swung open and out came one, two, three, four little sisters sprinting up the hill – one after the other. Their clothes were dirty and their hair hadn't been combed.

"Oh, no!" I thought. Now she'll know how much I needed the money.

"Thank you," I said, scurrying to get out of the car before my sisters gathered around. I shut the door in a hurry.

"O Jesus!" Excruciating pains shot up my left arm. Had she stabbed my hand? I started to run away, but couldn't. I looked down and saw my thumb trapped in the car door. I tried to pull my hand away, but that only increased the pain. What a dumb accident! "I'm stuck!"

"Oh, my gosh! What's the matter?" Mrs. O'Leary said. She stared at me like she was afraid that I'd gone crazy.

I panicked at the thought of losing my thumb. Then I got upset because I hadn't escaped before she saw me cry. I forgot about her and yelled, "Help!"

Mr. O'Leary came over and opened the rear car door and set my thumb free. The nail had a diagonal split like the slash in a percent sign.

"Are you all right?" Mrs. O'Leary said, sounding like she had a heart after all.

"Yes ma'am," I said. "Thank you." I went toward the house examining the dark line that was beginning to get bloody beneath my nail. My finger was throbbing as my little sisters walked beside me, saying, "Let me see, let me see."

Mr. O'Leary had already backed the car out of the driveway when I remembered my suitcase. I glanced back and saw Vera carrying my bag. She made me feel better. My little sisters loved me, even if Mrs. O'Leary thought I was a nobody.

How did she know the truth about my age? I thought I tricked her into hiring me, but I only fooled myself. I concluded that my smashed thumb was punishment for lying.

"Did you have a good time?" Mama asked as I handed her the twenty-dollar bill.

"Thank God it only lasted six days. I wouldn't have seen my sixteenth birthday if I'd been born back in slavery time. I would have run away or gotten myself killed. Thank you for the time of my birth."

"Tell me why you was crying outside," she said.

"I got caught in the lie about my age, and it hurt so bad." I showed her my split nail. I thought she'd say, "I told you so," but she didn't.

"Well, how did it go down at Myrtle Beach?" she said.

Mama wasn't going to leave me alone until I told her she was right about them people tricking me.

I shook my head at my own ignorance and shook my hand to ease my throbbing, aching thumb. "I said I worked like a slave."

Mama laughed. "What'd they make you do?"

"Clean up behind everybody and go hungry. That's what I did. I can't believe I was dumb enough to think I was going to have fun at the beach while babysitting. I wonder how slaves tolerated inferior treatment their whole lifetime without fighting back. Now I know why Ruth Brown sang, 'Mama he treats your daughter mean, he's the meanest man I've ever seen'."

Mama sang with me and then said, "That ain't 'bout slav'ry. She was singing 'bout her old man. Now you understand why I don't have a husband no more."

"I know I understand why black people eat fatback, chicken feet, pig ears, chitterlings, and such. That's all that was left after massa's family ate all the good food."

"But you learned to 'preciate anything you got, huh?"

"I sure did. But I asked God to explain to me why some dogs eat better than human beings. I don't understand that."

"Lemme know when you get the answer," she said.

"I will. But right now, I'm scared to get another job and get walked on like dirt because I'm black.

"You know all white folks ain't like them people. Some's nicer than colored folk."

Chapter 15

FROM LAUGHING TO MOURNING

THE SUN WAS PEEKING THROUGH the pines at six o'clock on the August morning that I began tenth grade. Standing beside Cashmere Road, giggling on the inside about going to high school, I tried to appear calm so I could look like a cool young lady. High school, the last leg of my academic journey!

My favorite expression from ninth grade French class crept into my head as the stop sign on the bus went out amid flashing lights that demanded attention. Pour moi? The bus stopped a few feet away. I felt extra special as I boarded, like I was moving up in the world. Too bad Mrs. O'Leary couldn't see me. She treated me like I was a dog, but a whole busload of people and cars traveling in both directions had stopped just for me. Never again will anybody mistreat me like that woman did. Never!

Noises were in the air. Geese honked, a rooster crowed, dogs barked. Why do animals get up so early when they don't have to go to school?

I plopped down in a middle seat in front of Erick and Gerald, two boys that loved to talk about football tryouts and taking back the championship trophy from Booker T. Washington High School.

"Don't you guys even care about your classes?" I said.

"Coach says we have to pay to play," Erick said. "So we pay our respects to the teachers by going to class and then play ball."

"High school students should value their education," I said.

"School would be so boring if we didn't have football," Gerald said. "My favorite classes are lunch, Band, Driver's Ed, and PE. Take them away and I might as well stay home to slop the hogs or milk the cow."

"How 'bout sampling food in Home Ec and music appreciation?" Erick said, slapping his fat thighs. His hams were as big a hog's and sounded like drums. He started singing Hambone.

"Hambone, hambone have you heard, papa's gonna buy me a bottle of wine. And if that bottle of wine get broke, papa's gonna grab my neck and choke. Hambone."

He grabbed his neck and pretended to be choking. People laughed. Then he beat his hams a few times before pointing to Gerald in the seat across the aisle.

"Hambone, hambone have you heard, papa's gonna buy me a BB gun," Gerald sang. "And if that BB gun don't shoot, papa's gonna kick me with his boot, and if that kick makes me break wind, papa's gonna peel off my black skin. Hambone."

"Ya'll cut it out!" the bus driver hollered.

People snickered but Hambone was shut down. Everybody knew better than to disturb the driver after he told us to hush. That would be a ticket to principal's office.

The big yellow bus rumbled on to the next stop where Elaine, my best friend, got on and sat beside me.

"The fellows behind us are ready to play sports," I said. "And I'm ready to spend the next three years at Madison High."

"Get used to hearing them talk," Elaine said. "Those big little boys can talk spots off a dog."

"I believe you," I said, giggling at her audacity to say whatever came to mind. I leaned my head against the window and watched treetops fly by as I drew a success plan for the whole school year in my mind. Hearing football jocks that didn't care about learning talk success on the first day made me think I should be just as positive.

I decided to read all the way to school. I'd use my extra thirty minutes after we arrived to complete homework that I didn't finish in study hall, and sleep on the long ride home. I'd make the honor roll and do my duty to keep the principal off my booty.

I implemented my plan and it worked well until the day in November when I saw my first report card. I had a 'C' in chemistry. It was the first low grade I'd ever made in school. Knowing I deserved better than that, I stared at it in disbelief. I'd done everything the teacher assigned. He was going to explain how I got that grade, or else I was going to report him for staying out of class when he should have been working.

On the bus ride home that Thursday afternoon, I was busy planning how to protest the grade Mr. Glass had given me. I didn't like him and I didn't like his class because he walked out every day while we answered questions at the end of the chapter and studied that drab green Periodic Table of Elements that I hated. Nobody in the class understood why we had to memorize it. How would it help us get a job? The teacher didn't even know.

I sat in chemistry class on Friday afternoon, getting angrier and angrier at Mr. Glass as he called the roll. At the end of class I was going to tell him that he made a mistake on my grade. All my other grades were A's and B's.

"Good afternoon," he said. His speech was slurred and his lips moist like a drunk. "Work on the Periodic Table of Elements and I'll be back in a few minutes."

I was fuming when he slid out the door. As soon as it slammed shut behind him, I blurted out, "I can't believe I got a 'C' in this class!"

"I got a 'C,' too, and I'm glad about it," Gerald said. "I did exactly none of the homework."

"Who got an 'A' or 'B' in this class?" I said.

Nobody answered.

"Raise your hand if you got a 'C,'" Gerald shouted, his hand already in the air. I looked around the classroom and saw everybody's hand raised.

Something was seriously wrong and I planned to find out what, as soon as Mr. Glass returned. But I leaned back in my seat and prepared to watch the boys mimic the teacher's slurred speech like they often did.

Cool Chester fell out of his chair and hollered "Ohhh!" He placed his pencil behind his ear, cleared his throat, and said, "Hmmm... today, Class, I'm stepping out for a shot of Jack Daniels because my wife just died and my son ran away from home because he was having trouble understanding Chemistry and, and, oh, let me tell you the truth, I hate my job!"

Everybody clapped when he finished. He bowed then looked around for the next speaker. Butch jerked his neck around like it was made out of rubber. Then he flashed his chipped front tooth as he pressed both hands on the desk and got up like he was having a hard time standing. "Well, uh, uh, I must admit that I'm justified in drinking at this hour of the day 'cause I just found out my wife's been cheating on me with my best friend. I wondered why my buddy was always singing "Who's Loving You?" and now I know why. I feel like such a fool! Somebody tell me how the Miracles knew my wife didn't love me no more and got the nerve to sang a song about it."

Laughter and clapping popped like an explosion. The class was loud.

Even though I was angry with Mr. Glass, I couldn't help laughing at the boys.

Mr. Glass rushed back to class a few minutes later, panting like somebody was chasing him.

"There's been a shooting!" He mumbled. He sashayed to the back of the lab where he turned on the wall-mounted black and white television set.

"A Roman Catholic priest had been called to administer the last rites," Walter Cronkite said. Seeing his worried face, I forgot all about being angry with Mr. Glass. "President John Fitzgerald Kennedy, the thirty-fifth president of the United States, is not expected to recover from a gunshot wound."

I think we all stopped breathing when we saw our president in that convertible. Some people started sniffling. I didn't know what to think. It was a real shooting, not a television show in which people get killed and come back to life in the next episode. My heart beat faster. I didn't understand all the talk about last rites and why Mr. Cronkite made the event sound like it was important to the whole world.

Then the principal, Mr. Wright, announced over the PA system: "Attention students and staff, I'm sorry to announce that President John F. Kennedy has been assassinated in Dallas, Texas. You are being dismissed early. Buses will be leaving in ten minutes. We need everyone, and I do mean everyone, to quickly and quietly evacuate the building in an orderly fashion. And please pray for our country."

"Comfort President Kennedy's wife and two small children, John and Caroline," I silently prayed while gathering my books. After getting stuck in the traffic jam at the door, I blurted, "Our president was a good man. He didn't deserve to die like that any more than I deserved a 'C' in this class. God, why did you let this happen? Why are we going home early? What can people in Columbia do about the president being shot in Dallas?"

Several classmates snapped at me all at once as people pushed and shoved.

"Duh! Because he's the president of the United States! And South Carolina is in the United States! They think a war will jump off! Because nobody's running the country!" Students yelled out all kinds of answers. They seemed angry enough to bite my head off. I thought it was a valid question, but I wished I hadn't said it so loud.

"You're leaving to show respect for the president," Mr. Glass slobbered.

The teacher's answer made sense to me, but as I watched students run toward the door, I still didn't understand the urgency of leaving school. Was it safer to be in a school bus with a student driver? Maybe they're trying to get us home as soon as possible just in case America goes to war. That was a scary thought.

Once outside the classroom, I ran down two flights of stairs toward the exit. Alphonso, our bus driver, responded to the national emergency in a way that helped me to understand why only responsible juniors and seniors could have his job. He sat calmly behind the wheel with the engine running and watched our sullen faces parade past him. His bus interior was blanketed with silence. He waited until we were all seated before he inched into the long line of buses that were pulling out of Madison High's parking lot. It felt like we were traveling in a funeral procession.

Although I really didn't understand how the assassination affected us, the early dismissal from school, the silence on the school bus, the tears, and the intermittent sniffling made me realize that the event was very serious. We definitely showed respect for our president. Never before had the bus been so quiet.

My ride home was filled with questions. When painful or puzzling events happen, how will I understand if I don't ask questions? The boys who snapped at me for asking were the same ones that made up speeches about Mr. Glass' alcohol consumption. They didn't even try to learn the truth about why his speech was slurred. Why are some people so quick to jump to conclusions? Why do they get annoyed with people like me who sincerely want to know rather than speculate? Why can't I forget their hurtful words?

Tears crept out of the corner of my closed eyes as I asked myself a lot of questions while riding along. I had no idea that my curiosity would benefit me one day.

Chapter 16
SWEET SIXTEEN

AFTER A BUSY EVENING OF LOOKING after little children, I wrote a letter to my sister Lynette, the only person who understood my feelings.

Dear Lynette, Knowing it didn't bother John F. Kennedy to be the first Catholic president—a big thing according to Walter Cronkite— made me think I could be the first person in our family to do something unusual. Having a birthday party would be huge for me. The president died young, but it was after he'd achieved a goal. If I have to die young, I pray it will be after, and not before, I celebrate my sixteenth birthday. For once in my life, I'd like to know what it feels like to be treated special. I miss you. Say hello to Beverly.

Ten days after I mailed the letter, I found a card from New York in the mailbox. Inside, wrapped in aluminum foil, were two twenties and a five-dollar bill. Lynette had written: *Merry Christmas and Happy Birthday! Turning sweet sixteen is very special. We want you to celebrate any way you choose. Thinking of you with love, Lynette ($25) and Beverly ($20).*

Beverly knew I didn't like getting one present for two occasions. It wasn't my fault I was born two days after Christmas. But this time, I didn't mind getting a combination gift. Forty-five dollars was more than enough for one present.

While stuffing the cash back in the envelope, my favorite French term, *pour moi,* came to mind. All this money was just for me. I decided not to tell Mama about it because she might ask to borrow.

"Celebration time is here," I told myself. Ideas for

a square dance jamboree twirled around in my head, so I pretended to do-si-do my partner as I ran inside the house. I hid the envelope where nobody would ever find it, beneath piles of summer clothes in the bottom of the chifforobe.

Then I decided to give myself a big party on my birthday. Why wait until Saturday when Friday is my big day? The president's assassination proved that tomorrow is not promised to anybody.

I addressed a stack of personal invitations two weeks before my party. The theme was *Party Lights in the Night: Can you dig it?* Inside the invitations I wrote, "Come and join me for the birthday celebration of a lifetime on Friday, December 27th from seven o'clock until…" I giggled as I anticipated people's surprise reaction to receive a card from me.

I gave everybody on the school bus and all the teenagers at church an invitation. I drew a star on each little red envelope, and wrote the date inside to emphasize that the party was during the Christmas break. I was the star and so were they. I knew many of them lived too far to come, but at least they couldn't say I hadn't invited them.

On Friday morning, the day of my sixteenth birthday, I promised my brother Harry a dollar if he'd go to the store with me to help carry party supplies. He would be the iceman.

"Why do you need to have a party when you know how old you are?" Harry said. "We never had a birthday party in this family before."

"That's my point," I said. "A birthday party makes you feel special. The presents I get will help me remember the day I turned sixteen. Besides, I'm tired of hearing other people talk about celebrating every year and I've never done it."

"Oh, okay, sis," he said. "Have it your way."

Loaded with forty dollars, my black pleather pocketbook swung on my cocked arm as Harry and I walked to the bus stop. I felt like a proud millionaire taking my hired help along for the ride. I kept wondering who would come to share my food and fun and what kind of presents they would bring.

We caught the early morning bus and got off at Winn Dixie, five miles away. My plan was to return home around one o'clock. That would give me all afternoon to get everything ready for the party.

Harry pushed the shopping cart through the aisles while I tossed in a Happy Birthday banner, red balloons, plates, cups, napkins, both Lays and Wise potato chips, sugar, cherry Kool-aid, lemons, hot dogs, buns, catsup, mustard, cookies, and a bag of ice.

At the check out counter, I pulled out my forty dollars and paid the total bill of $27.54. After getting my change, I paid Harry his dollar and put the rest away. We returned to the bus stop and set the bags down on the sidewalk to wait for the bus.

"I'm so glad I estimated correctly," I said. "I'll have money left over after I pay for my cake. That way my pocketbook won't feel empty. I hope the ice won't melt before we get home."

"Maybe we'll catch a ride," Harry said, as the bus stopped in front of us. Twenty minutes later we were walking down Cashmere Road when my classmate Bobbie Sue's grandpa, Mr. Zack, pulled up next to us and stopped his black Chrysler. He looked like a little boy clutching a big steering wheel with both hands.

"Goody, a ride!" I said.

Harry hopped in behind the driver while I ran around to the passenger side. "Thank you," I said, pushing my bag to the middle of the backseat so I could get in.

"C'mon up here and show me how to git to yo house," the old man barked.

I shut the rear door and then jumped in the front on the end of the long bench seat. Mr. Zack, about eighty years old, drove straight ahead. "Thank you so much for giving us a lift," I said.

He grunted.

I stared out the windshield as we rode in silence.

A few minutes later, I glanced at the speedometer. It read 20 miles per hour. "He must think he's driving faster than he is," I thought. "Oh well. Riding feels good. I'll get home in plenty of time to get ready."

Something plopped down on my thigh. I looked down and saw Mr. Zack's shriveled hand pushing up my denim skirt. He didn't seem to notice, so I brushed his hand away and he gripped the steering wheel with it.

"Rest your hand on the seat, not on me," I wanted to say, thinking he had mistaken my thigh for the seat.

"Gimme summa dat trim," he said.

"What?" I said, thinking he'd asked for some of the food in our grocery bag. I glanced at the bags on the backseat beside Harry. My brother was staring out the side window like he hadn't heard a thing.

Without saying a word, I turned my head and looked straight ahead.

Mr. Zack reached over and put his hand on my thigh again.

"Gimme summa dat trim," he said.

I turned and stared at him.

He grinned at me, showing both his top and bottom gums.

My body stiffened when the puny old man stared at me like a toothless shark about to attack. I felt trapped. He's lost his mind.

Without thinking about it, I opened the car door and jumped out. I rolled along the hard ground until I came to a stop in the ditch beside the road. With Harry in the backseat, the car rolled on down the road like I'd never been in it.

I got up, brushed off my clothes, wiped my face with my palms and felt relieved when I didn't see blood anywhere. Sobbing, I started walking and praying. "God, I could have been killed. But you didn't let me get hurt at all. That old coot tried to ruin my birthday! P-l-e-a-s-e, p-l-e-a-s-e let Harry and my food get home okay. You know I've been looking forward to this party for a long time. Please don't let me be disappointed."

Harry ran outside to meet me when I turned into the path in front of our house.

"Sis, why did you jump out the car like that? He brought me home with the food."

"You wouldn't understand that a girl's got to fight for her safety and sanity," I said. "Anyhow, I'm glad you got home safely. I could have been killed and you didn't have a clue."

"You opened the door and jumped out yourself," Harry said. "Did you want to commit suicide on your birthday?'

"Heck no!" I said. "It would be a terrible thing to die young and never have really lived. All I wanted to do today was to enjoy my birthday party."

I felt like I was going to burst out crying so I left Harry standing outside. I went into the bathroom and examined my hair and face for bruises. When I was younger, I'd thought growing up would be fun. But today I learned that little people have little problems and big people have big problems. Why did I have to struggle so hard when I tried to do the right thing?

"Whew! No bruises," I said after examining myself in the bathroom mirror and pulling pine needles out of my hair. "Thank God nothing worse happened to me today."

In the kitchen, I heated two big pots of water for a warm bubble bath. While waiting, Vera and I blew up red balloons in the living room. We laughed as one of her tied balloons crawled open and made a funny noise while the air escaped.

"You blow and I'll tie," I said, taking a big spool of white thread from Mama's sewing basket. I used it to make a knot on the end of each balloon as soon as it was inflated. "Take them up to the house," I told Vera. "When you come back, please put on a pot of water and boil the wieners while I take a bath."

"Okay," she said. "I'm glad to help. Getting ready for a party is fun." She wrapped the loose strings once around her wrist and went out the front door clutching the strings at the other end.

"Be careful not to burst them," I shouted as she ran up the hill to our old house.

I took the special clothes I'd saved for my special day into the bathroom and laid them on the lid on the commode, but my dress, I hung on the nail behind the door.

I sprinkled two heaping tablespoons of bubble bath in the tub and dumped two buckets of cold water in before pouring in the two pots of boiling hot water. The scent of strawberries filled the tiny bathroom. I thought of the times I used to stretch out in a bathtub half full of water but later had to stand up in a round tin tub. How glad I was to be able to stretch out my legs.

"Thank God for little things like a real bathtub with a drain in the bottom," I murmured as I squeezed the yellow sponge and water rolled down my back.

After drying off, I dusted my chest with the powder puff from a fresh box of lilac and put on the pretty red satin dress with chiffon around the skirt that Mama had made for me. I combed and brushed my hair and then patted down the bangs that swirled over my forehead. Finally, I dabbed a little Emeraude perfume behind both ears. Beautiful Me!

I must have twirled around ten times in front of the full-length mirror nailed to the back of the door before leaving the bathroom. The heels on my black leather pumps clapped with approval as I strolled back across the hardwood floors.

"Oh my goodness!" Vera said when I stepped into the kitchen to check on the hot dogs. "You look like a storybook princess!"

"I feel like one too," I said. "I'm ready for this party."

We gathered all the party supplies and went to the empty house next door to finish decorating. I had just stepped down off a chair after hanging the Happy

Birthday banner over the door of what used to be the children's bedroom in the house, when Erick, my first guest arrived.

Erick walked in while Vera was placing the hot dogs and all the trimmings on a folding table covered with a red tablecloth. I'd given him ten dollars to have his mother bake a yellow birthday cake with coconut icing, and write "Happy Birthday Davida" on it in big red letters. I was so pleased when I saw that she had added decorations of red maraschino cherries on top. My cake made a perfect centerpiece.

The sight of balloons and a cake with my name on it made me forget all about the frightening incident that had happened earlier with Mr. Zack.

"Nothing is going to spoil this day!" I whispered. "Nothing!"

Soon all of the teenagers from Cashmere Road started piling into our old house at the top of the hill. Gerald, my disc jockey, played all of the latest hit songs. My favorites were "Fingertips" by Little Stevie Wonder, "Two Lovers" by Mary Wells, and "For Your Precious Love" by Jerry Butler, The Iceman.

I must have danced about ten times to Claudine Clark's song, "Party Lights," and with every boy at least once or twice. We did the Watusi, the Swim, the Loco-Motion, the Twist, the Cha-Cha, the Monkey, the Mash Potato, the Funky Chicken, the Hully Gully, and the Limbo Rock. The only dance I didn't do was the Dog, because it looked too nasty.

The room was full of body heat. During a moment when I came up for air, I picked up a brown paper bag and fanned hot air and musty odor. Perspiration rolled down my back.

"Getting drenched proves you really know how to get your grove on, girl," I told myself. How exhilarating!

Seeing boys peel off their colorful Ban-Lon tops, showing their white T-shirts, reminded me of the story in the Bible that says David honored the Lord by dancing out of his clothes, but he didn't get butt naked. Dancing frees people to cast aside all cares and just do their own thing. God must approve of it because people dance in the church.

"One more spin of the wax before you move on down the tracks?" My disc jockey hollered. It felt like we were just starting to have fun for real. "Last song!" he said again before putting another 45 on the turntable. Every time people started to leave they turned back and danced some more.

A minute past midnight Elaine shouted, "That's it! Stop the music!

"Thanks for coming," I said, as people left the room.

Elaine shooed everybody out. She was the last to leave. As we walked together in the chilly night air toward Cashmere Road, I told her that my greatest wish had come true.

"I can't decide which was more fun, the planning or the party," I said. "Now I know what a sweet sixteen birthday party is like. Even if I never have another one I'll remember this night for the rest of my life."

"I'm glad you got your wish," she said. "People acted like they never wanted to go home. That's the sign of a good party you know."

It felt good to celebrate my own accomplishments without waiting for someone else to acknowledge me. At last, I knew how it felt to be the birthday girl. I didn't receive one gift, but I wasn't a bit surprised. Everybody I knew who was born around Christmas got cheated out of presents. Even when my daddy gave me a gift, he always said, "Merry Christmas and Happy Birthday!"

"You looked like Cinderella at the ball when everybody sang happy birthday to you," Elaine said. "You were blushing. You knew you looked good."

"I felt like Cinderella at the ball," I said. "That song made my day. Did you see how my guests ate and drank everything and looked for more?"

"That means they had a good time," she said.

"I wished the evening would last forever," I said.
"Now I can't wait to see what's in store for me as a sixteen
year old."

Chapter 17

A CHANGING CLIMATE

AFTER CHRISTMAS BREAK, I RETURNED to Madison High in January 1965 eager to enroll in Distributive Education (DE). The new elective was designed to prepare students for the changing job market in Columbia, South Carolina.

One day, Mrs. Steele, the light-skinned DE teacher with brown crinkled hair, turned to me during her lecture. "Davida, would you please consider joining our new chapter of the Distributive Education Clubs of America known as DECA? You have tremendous leadership skills and you know how to take care of business."

Without waiting for my response, she turned to the class and said, "I urge all of you who would desire employment to take advantage of this opportunity. At sixteen you can legally get a job. Our city is changing, and there are many benefits in joining DECA."

My teacher had given me a whole new perspective of myself. She'd encouraged me to see who I could become, rather than remaining a poor student who desperately needed a job. She cared about us, and our future, not just the subject she taught. She made me feel like a young woman, blossoming, as the real me unfolded. I was willing to do whatever she recommended.

"I'd like to join DECA, but I ride the school bus and there's no way for me to get home if we meet after school," I said.

"Good. We'll plan to meet either before school or during lunch," she said. "That will work better for me, too."

Excited as I left the room, I punched my fist into the air, pretending I was knocking down all the obstacles that might hinder my advancement. "I'm going to get a regular job!" I said.

The following day, Mrs. Steele announced a round-table discussion in her classroom at lunchtime. I ate quickly then rushed to the meeting.

"The first thing we need to do is to elect officers," she told the group of twelve students who showed up.

"I say let Davida be president," a boy blurted.

"I think Davida is the best one for the job," a girl said.

"Well, how many would agree to have Davida serve as the first president?" Mrs. Steele asked.

The other eleven students raised their hands.

"Davida is our president by unanimous vote," she said.

"Thank you for your confidence in me," I said. "I'll do my best." They chose me! I wanted to holler, but I remained calm. I couldn't wait to go home and tell Mama.

"The segregated climate in Columbia is changing," Mrs. Steele said. "In fact, non-traditional jobs are opening up even as we speak. Jobs are becoming available this year that have never before existed for Colored people. You students are on the cutting edge of these changes. If you are willing to work, then I will submit your name, and the NAACP will support me in my efforts to help you to secure employment."

"I'm ready to work anywhere I can get a job," I blurted, raising my hand. While the teacher wrote my name, I wondered how I'd get home at night without transportation.

All of the other students in the group said they had to wait until they talked to their parents.

That's their problem, not mine. Mama needs all the help she can get.

"Very well then, just let me know tomorrow," she said. "Meanwhile I'll get to work on Davida's request right away. We need someone to make a motion to adjourn the meeting."

"So moved," I said. Having practiced Roberts Rules of order, I showed everybody that their president could speak up.

"I second that emotion… I mean that motion," a boy said. We laughed when he quoted Smokey Robinson.

"The meeting is adjourned," Mrs. Steele said. "Davida, you will preside at all future meetings."

"Yes ma'am."

On the way out, I began singing "I don't want nobody to give me nothing, just open up the door, I'll get it myself." Other students joined in until one boy hollered, "I feel good!" like James Brown.

DE, a different kind of class, put education in the head and in the hands.

***

Mrs. Steele arranged an interview for me at Sears Roebuck and Company in the Sears Town Shopping Center. "It will be a milestone in the city's history if you get the job," she said. "You've got to look confident and determined the moment they lay eyes on you. Have an air about you that lets the interviewer know that you're the best candidate for the position."

While I absorbed every gesture and every word, she held her head high and strutted back and forth across the floor like she owned the place.

Something important was happening. I knew it when she insisted that I practice for the interview every day.

"You've got to be better than all the other job applicants," she said. "This is a competition, and you're there to win. You must sit, stand, shake hands, speak correctly, maintain eye contact, answer interview questions, tell them you will work in any department, and be polite even if someone makes a scathing racial comment like, 'Some of my best friends are black.' Smile and show them you're not easily offended. Remember, this type of interview is new for them, too."

"I've got everything memorized down to a tee," I said the day before the interview. But Mrs. Steele interviewed me anyway, one last time.

"Perfect!" she said, clapping like her own child had just scored a touchdown. "Do that tomorrow. Be sure to thank the interviewer for his time before you leave."

The next morning, Mrs. Steele waited in the car while I sat in my eleven o'clock job interview, dressed in a two-piece brown suit. I felt cute with my legs crossed at the ankle.

A gray-haired man with a gray mustache invited me to sit in a chair opposite his mahogany desk. He and a tall red-haired man waited for me to sit before they sat down.

"Thank you for your interest in working at Sears Roebuck and Company," the old man said, from behind his desk. He talked about how the company started when Sears bought watches and hired a watch repairman named Roebuck. "Did you know that Mr. Roebuck had dark-skinned English parents?" he said.

"No sir, I wasn't aware of that fact," I said calmly. He'd surprised me with that question, but I was ready for the rest.

"Most people don't know that, either," he said, then continued telling me the company history. He concluded with, "Sears bought out Roebuck and kept his name." He looked at the red-haired man and said, "Mr. Solomon is going to tell you about the toy department."

I maintained good eye contact and even smiled a few times as he talked about all the money people spend on toys, especially train sets. When Mr. Solomon finished talking, the old man said, "Give her a tour of the toy department."

"Come with me," Mr. Solomon said. He looked like Santa's grown up elf as his long red sleeve flapped in the air when he beckoned me.

"Welcome to Sears Roebuck," the old man said. "After your tour, you are free to leave."

"Thank you, sir," I said. Did that mean I had the job?

Mr. Solomon held the door for me to exit first. Then I followed him to the escalator and stood one step behind him. Why did they only talk about Sears and the toy department? When was he going to ask all the questions we practiced?

"You'll like working here," he said, turning toward me. "I've been in the toy department for twenty-three years and I just love it."

"Do I have the job?" I asked.

"You sure do," he said with a big smile. "I knew you had the job when you first opened your mouth to speak. You present yourself very well. Congratulations!"

"Thank you, sir."

My heart turned a somersault. I was sooo happy. I took mental notes of every detail when he showed me row after row familiar and brand new toys. The job sounded too easy to be true. I had to put toys out, help people find them, and then ring up the sale on a cash register. That was all he expected me to do.

"We're in a great location here at the end of the building," he said. "With the parking lot next to us, people stop to look when they enter or when they leave. We get the most foot traffic at Sears Town. Well, that's it until you report for work next week."

"I'll see you next week," I said. "Thank you again." We shook hands and I walked outside and then skipped back to the car saying, "I got the job! I got the job!"

"I knew it," Mrs. Steele said. "I just knew it! I'm glad the interviewers were smart enough to know it, too."

***

Mr. Solomon taught me the toy business my first night on the job. He took me in a back room to see the employee entrance and the time clock. He stopped by a metal machine attached to the wall, found my name on a card, and said, "Every time you come in, look for your time card in one of these slots. He handed me my card and said, "Go on and put the card in the time clock and listen for the click."

Seeing my name typed on a card was special. I clocked in at seventeen hundred hours while Mr. Solomon observed. I'd wondered why we needed to learn military time in math class. Now I knew. Every little detail seemed important to me.

"Put the card back in the slot and be sure to punch out the same way," he said. "Payroll picks up cards every week and puts out new ones. Your pay envelope will be ready for pick up every Thursday. One more thing, that stockroom full of boxes on skids, belongs to the toy department. If we run out of stock, check back here before you say we don't have an item."

"Yes, sir," I said.

"Be sure to put on a red smock in that room over there before you report to the register," he said.

I grabbed a small smock and put it on before following him through swinging double doors into the toy department. We walked side-by-side down every aisle.

"Our most popular toys are Barbie, G.I. Joe, and train sets," he said. "You'll have to remember where everything is on every shelf, in every aisle. When you can't find a toy on the shelf, ask the customer to please wait while you check for it in the stockroom. That's all you need to know. You'll see that it won't take long to be a pro in the toy business. Do you have any questions?"

I laughed. "Not right now. But I'm sure I'll have plenty later on."

"The schedule changes every week so just call the store on Monday, give your name and ask when you should come in. I'll show you the break room when it's your turn. I'll teach you how to use the cash register and show you how to watch out for counterfeit bills. Your primary job is to smile and ask customers, 'May I help you, please?' "

Then he got serious and fixed his gray eyes on me as though to look deep into my heart.

"If a customer refuses your offer to help, be polite and say, 'Just a minute.' Then go get someone else. Everyone won't receive your help."

"I'll do that," I said.

I soon understood Mr. Solomon's warning. My first night at work, a man and a woman barked at me like I was a dog that had entered their yard. Their young son called me the "N" word. Then a thin gray-haired woman with deep wrinkles like railroad tracks across her face shouted, "No Niggra! You may not help me!" She kept on fussing loudly, even after I walked away to get Mr. Solomon.

He rushed over to her saying, "How can I help you?"

Immediately, some of her wrinkles flattened out like his words pressed them with a hot iron.

"Nat King Cole probably sang, 'Smile, though your heart is aching / smile, even though it's breaking' because he experienced racial discrimination, too," I thought.

I smiled and did as Mr. Solomon advised, even though I felt that some people deserved a good old-fashioned booty whuppin' like Daddy used to give us. My boss never talked about the customers who acted ugly. But I understood why. They were his people. The few black people that shopped for toys were surprised to see me.

Mr. Solomon showed me how to place orders when stock was low and how to balance the register at the end of the night. In a short time, I became proficient in the toy business.

"You catch on quickly," he said one night after I'd been working a month. "I'm going to make sure to put you on the schedule for at least two days every week so you can always have a pay envelope to pick up on Thursday night."

Mrs. Steele was so happy about my employment success that she arranged an appearance on WIS television for eight o'clock one Saturday morning. She found out that I was the first black salesgirl in Columbia when the State newspaper published an article about me that included my picture.

"I'd like for you to appear on television along with other chapter presidents to talk about our goals and accomplishments," she said. "I'll get you a DECA blazer to wear to the television interview so everyone can see that we are serious about coming together as a unified club. I just need you to be committed to go and represent us."

On Friday, she presented me with a navy blue wool blazer with DECA embroidered in gold letters on the front pocket. "This will match whatever you decide to wear," she said.

Saturday morning I dressed in a cute denim dress I'd purchased using my ten percent employee discount. After admiring my chic blazer in the mirror, I headed out the door at six o'clock. Mrs. Steele had said, "Wear your DECA blazer so people will recognize this great program." Determined to make my teacher proud of me, I walked six miles to the bus stop in Ridgewood because the Cashmere Road city bus started running too late for me to reach WIS on time.

When I arrived at the television station, I pulled the glass door, but it was locked. I knocked, but nobody answered. Had I done all that walking and rushing in vain? A telephone booth was on the corner but the book was missing, and I didn't have a number to call Mrs. Steele or WIS. At eight-thirty I knew I had failed to accomplish my goal of representing my DECA group on television. But just in case I'd made a mistake about the time, I stood in front of the building until nine o'clock. Seeing no sign of life outside or inside, I spent the rest of the morning window shopping and daydreaming about owning a big wardrobe.

Monday morning, before I could explain what happened, Mrs. Steele said she received word late Friday night that the television interview had been postponed.

I groaned. If only somebody had called me. She had no idea what I had endured to make it to the station on time.

"I hope it wasn't too much of an inconvenience," she said.

Speechless, I smiled. She didn't know I walked across town to work and then walked around in the toy department for two, three or four hours a night.

Within a few months, Mr. Solomon had promoted me to lead salesclerk. In the fall, he made me responsible for training new hires for the Christmas season. Customers who rejected my help got to see white sales clerks come to me for assistance. I gloated as I gave instructions amid scowls on their faces. I savored the sweet taste of vengeance.

When I worked alone in the toy department, white customers often took their purchases elsewhere rather than allow me to ring up the sale. They incorrectly assumed that I was working on commission. I understood that they were not accustomed to being assisted by a Negro salesgirl. "How many times must a white clerk come and ask me for the stock number or how to ring up an item before they understand that I know what I'm doing? I hate it when people put on airs in public. Some of them that go overboard to hurt my feelings have black people in their home cooking, cleaning, and babysitting. They ought to be ashamed of themselves for acting so ugly," I thought.

It was a pleasure working under Mr. Solomon, a white man who showed compassion for me, and one who knew his own people very well. I was extremely impressed the first time he called a team meeting and asked, "How do you think we can increase toy sales?"

"We could open on Sunday during the Christmas season," I said.

"You're right," he said, "but the store can't do that because South Carolina's Blue Laws prohibit the sale of non-food items on Sunday."

"Then give people more time to shop. Keep only the toy department open until ten or eleven on Friday or Saturday night."

"That's a great idea!" he said, and wrote it down.

Unaware that he had entered my idea in the company's new suggestion box, I was shocked a week later when he handed me an envelope containing the twenty-dollar reward. He treated me like I was his daughter. I liked him.

Some customers snubbed me during The Midnight Toy Extravaganza held four Saturdays before Christmas. I wanted to tell them it was my idea that gave them the privilege of shopping late, but I didn't. I just ignored them and helped those who accepted me. Smiling when they frowned, I reflected on my starting pay of eighty-five cents per hour, getting a ten-cent raise one month later, and now earning a dollar and twenty-five cents per hour minimum wage even if I didn't sell a single toy. They'd really get the lockjaw if they knew that.

I felt pretty good about my progress considering Mama barely made two dollars a day (housekeepers didn't qualify for minimum wage). With my help, our family was rising out of poverty and I didn't have to work like a slave for the money either.

At work I proudly walked around in my red smock saying, "May I help you, please?" Following advice received from Mrs. Steele and Mr. Solomon, I responded to bigotry in a way that confused rude customers. They probably thought I was a dingbat when I said, "Thank you," whenever somebody called me *nigger, coon, niggra, darkie, spook,* or *blackie.* I just moved on or ignored the person. I knew some names like *whitey, cracker, honkey, redneck, paleface,* and *Mr. Charlie,* but saying them could get me fired. Turning the other cheek made me feel superior.

"Never give anyone the satisfaction of knowing they've insulted you if you can avoid it," Mrs. Steele had said. "Just be yourself and keep them guessing." That statement came to mind every time someone tried to insult me.

In one of our DECA meetings, I told how white people dropped change in my hand like they were afraid of turning black or catching a contagious disease if they touched me. "I don't get it. Nobody ever refused change from my black hand. Why do they think blacks are inferior to whites? Don't they know that money circulates from hand to hand all day long? What's wrong with them?"

"God doesn't show partiality, but people do," Mrs. Steele said. "Whenever you're mistreated, do what the Bible tells you in Matthew 5:44. Pray for those who persecute you. Desegregation is about lifting restrictions on where minorities can work and the types of jobs they can have, among other things. You are dealing with the public that finds it hard to accept seeing Colored people in non-traditional roles. Sears Roebuck is trying to do the right thing by putting you out front, but the new desegregation laws challenge all of us to change our perceptions of other racial groups. It won't happen overnight. But we must keep pace with these changing times."

My teacher was right. Change came when customers began asking me for help.

Chapter 18
JOB CHALLENGES

"I SHOLD DO THANK YOU," Mama said as I handed her a portion of the money I'd received in my pay envelope that night. "How do you like being sixteen?"

"It feels good to finally be old enough to work," I said. She was sitting at the sewing machine when I looked into her eyes and blurted, "I'm trying to help you around here, but you keep bringing more babies into this house."

"That's it for me. I had my tubes tied two years ago after Yvette was born."

"You did what?" I closed my eyes and then opened them to be sure it was my mama, the woman who popped out babies every year or two, who had said those words. "Did I hear right? You know this house is always noisy."

"You heard me," she said. "I don't know what to do with all these children."

Mama is talking to me about her feelings. "I thought I was the only one who was tired of you having babies," I said. "Oh, this is a night to remember!"

I'd planned to shout "Hallelujah!" when Yvette, Mama's last baby, turned three. Feeling great as I crawled under the blanket on my rollaway, I fluffed my feather pillow and tucked the blanket under my chin.

The next morning, screeching brakes on the bus sounded like music rather than noise. While the boys sang Hambone on the long bus ride to school, I thought about my daily routine. Every workday was a challenge. After school I had to walk two miles to my job. At work I walked around all night smiling at customers, but hoping and praying I'd get a ride home.

Not wanting to carry thick textbooks, and not having

thin ones like those we used in Sunday School that fit in my pocketbook, I did my assignments on the bus and in study hall. Sleep was all I wanted to do by the time I made it home at night.

While walking into the toy department a few nights after I began working there, I remembered my gift of a '58 Ford from my sister Lynette's husband. I'm sixteen now. I could get my car fixed, take the driver's test, get my license and not have to wait on anybody to bring me home. I went to the phone near the cash register and called Uncle Clyde, Mama's brother.

"I need Gray Goose repaired," I said. "I don't know why I never thought of repairing it before. Can you fix it?"

"My buddy, Woodrow, can do it. He's a shade tree mechanic. We'll talk about it later."

I thought Uncle Clyde meant that he and I would talk about it later. Instead, he and Mr. Woodrow came to our house on Saturday morning. They were outside working on Gray Goose when I woke up. I ran out in my pajamas just in time to hear my car hiccup, choke and die when he tried to start it, and then roar like a lion that had been asleep in the barn for almost two years.

"You did it! You did it! We've got a car! Yahoo!" I jumped up and down like a puppy trying to snatch a treat from its owner.

Uncle Clyde and Mr. Woodrow bumped shoulders to congratulate themselves. I guess they didn't want to shake their dirty hands. They laughed as though they were surprised at their own success.

"I prayed for my car to run, and God answered my prayer," I said.

I don't think they heard me. They jumped in Gray Goose and drove to the end of the driveway, backed the car up and stopped abruptly. Then they repeated the process. It was funny watching two grown men play like little boys.

When they finished working, I handed Uncle Clyde a twenty-dollar bill to pay his buddy, and then I slid in behind the wheel. "Thank you," I said. "I'm so happy I could cry."

"Go head and cry," Uncle Clyde said, laughing. "We won't stop you."

I sat there wondering what to do next. I needed a license, but without registration or insurance there was no way I could take the driver's test in Gray Goose. I thought and thought until I got an idea.

***

Monday morning when we arrived at school, I called my three friends Erick, Gerald and Frank aside to have a private talk.

"Would you guys be willing to take turns driving my car to pick me up from work?" I said.

"Yeah!" Gerald said without hesitation.

"Count me in," Frank said.

"Girl, you ask good questions on a Monday morning," Erick said. "Every boy I know would be glad to help you out with driving a car. I've got my license, but my daddy won't let me drive anything but his tractor. Drive a car. Wow! We can take turns. When it's my turn I'll just tell my ole' man I'm going somewhere with Harry."

"Then it's a deal?" I said. "I only ask that you be waiting outside the Toy Department at quitting time if you want to drive my car again. Is that fair?"

"Fair enough," they all said.

I dashed inside Madison High, leaving them outside to swap stories about how much fun they had the last time they drove. I didn't want to hear anything that might make me nervous about trusting them with my car.

***

When I got my work schedule for the week, I put my three drivers in a rotation and wrote down their assignments. Using Erick's idea, I asked my brother to help, too.

"Harry, I'm depending on you to drive the car to each driver's house one hour before time for me to get off work," I said. "I don't want them to have the car all day because they might get in trouble or burn up all my gasoline. Besides, I don't have any insurance on the car and the tags will soon expire. All they have to do is drive to Sears Town on Harden Street at night, pick me up, and then drive back home."

"I'll gladly do that, Sis," Harry said. "Thank you for letting me drive, too."

"I'm trusting you with Gray Goose. Don't hurt her." I tried not to remember that he had broken something two years ago when he hotwired my car and drove it.

The rotation worked out very well for several months. Then one night I went outside and my car wasn't there. I waited as long as I could and then ran to catch the last bus leaving downtown for Ridgewood. I prayed for a ride home as I walked toward Cashmere Road, but it didn't do any good. Most people were already in by ten o'clock at night. I stopped when I reached my classmate Naomi's house because I didn't want to walk past the church cemetery late at night.

I tapped on the front door of Naomi's house, afraid her parents might get upset with me for waking them up, but I swallowed my pride and took a chance that they'd let me in.

Someone came to the door and turned on the porch light. I was standing in front of the glass window in the door when the curtain moved.

"Who is it?" her mother, Mrs. Meyers, said.

"It's me, Davida," I whispered. "My ride didn't come to pick me up after work. I walked all the way from Ridgewood, and I'm so tired."

A top and bottom lock clicked and the door opened.

"You poor child," she said. "C'mon in. You can sleep on the sofa."

I locked the door behind me while she went into a

room. She came back carrying a blanket and spread it over the hard plastic cover on the couch.

"Lie down and rest here," she said.

"Thank you so much. I'll leave early so I can walk on home."

"Just lock the bottom lock behind you," she said.

Sleep came right away. I woke up around four o'clock, folded the blanket and then tiptoed out of the house.

When I got home, Harry greeted me with a loud, "I'm glad to see you, Sis. I'm sorry the car got stuck in the ditch. Something snapped underneath. I'll try to fix it after school today."

"Never mind!" I shouted as I ran to find something to wear to school. "You don't know what a rough night I had. I never want to be stranded like that again." I washed up, changed clothes, and headed for the school bus stop.

After school I called Mr. Woodrow to come over. With Harry's help, he pushed Gray Goose out of the ditch and into our driveway. It was fascinating to watch them push a car that weighed over a ton.

Seeing Mr. Woodrow push and run alongside the car with the door open and his hand on the steering wheel was scary. Then he jumped into the driver's seat of the rolling car and pressed the brakes when it reached the barn. He got out, crawled underneath the Ford on his back, and tinkered for a long time.

Hopeful like one of Perry Mason's clients, I waited for his "not guilty" verdict.

"What's the matter?" I said after his examination. "Can you fix it?"

"Broke an axle," he said. "Repairs will cost more than the car's worth."

"Oh no!" I groaned. I turned to Harry and glared at him. "Look what you did! You knew I was depending on you."

He dropped his head like he was sorry. That wasn't good enough for me because this wasn't the first time he had broken my car.

"How am I supposed to get home from work now?" I said, throwing my hands in the air to keep from slapping him. Accidents do happen, but all I could think of was, "Why me?"

"That'll be three dollars for me coming out here," Mr. Woodrow said, picking up his tools.

I couldn't believe he had the nerve to ask for pay when he hadn't fixed my car. I groaned again as I searched my pocketbook for the money. I felt like I was paying for nothing at all because Uncle Clyde wasn't there to speak up for me.

Angry, I fought hard to prevent tears from falling and my voice from cracking as I ran into the house, yelling, "Mama! Harry wrecked my car and now I don't know how I can get home from work. I might have to quit my job."

I didn't expect Mama to offer a solution. Usually she didn't offer advice unless I asked for it, but this time she gave me hope.

"Clyde works at Goodyear. Down the street from Sears Town," she said. "Ask him if he'll pick you up after he knocks off work."

"Really?" I said. I felt myself calm down. I called him at work.

"Uncle Clyde, my car stopped running again. Mr. Woodrow said repairing a broken axle will cost too much. Mama told me to ask if you will please pick me up and bring me home after you get off work. Can you help me?"

"Well, uh, uh, all right," he said. "But I don't get off 'til eight and sometimes nine. Call ahead of time and let me know what days and I'll pick you up. You might have to wait awhile if I have to work late."

"Oh thank you. I'll call you on Mondays."

Elated, I hung up the phone saying, "Yes! He said, Yes! Thanks Mama. He'll do it. I'll give him five dollars each week for gasoline even though he said I didn't have to pay him."

Mama never paid her brother to take her anywhere because she never had any extra money. But I knew it wasn't good for people to take their relatives for granted. Trucks need gas like the human body needs food. And a ride all the way to the country was a sacrifice, even for my uncle.

"Farewell, Gray Goose," I muttered as I stared through the living room window at my good-looking car that could start up, but couldn't move. "The car doctor pronounced you D-E-A-D. But I hate to see you go."

***

For the first few months, Uncle Clyde was waiting when I got off work. Then one night I was standing outside beneath a streetlight, staring at the empty parking lot, begging God to make my uncle remember me, when his pickup came speeding toward me.

"I thought you forgot about me," I said, climbing into the truck. I knew better than to fuss at him because he was doing me a favor.

"Almost! Time got away from me."

"Well I'm sure glad you caught up with it," I said.

After that, I called his job about ten minutes before their closing time to remind him I was working that night. Once I stepped outside the building, the doors were locked and there was no way to contact him.

I called to remind him one night, but he was late anyway. I waited and waited and begged God to make him come to get me. An hour later he still hadn't come. Not a single car came into the parking lot and only a few cars drove past. I panicked when I realized I was stranded. I didn't have a plan B to get home.

"Okay God, please tell me what to do now?" I said. I listened for an answer, but heard nothing but traffic on Harden Street. When I saw a city bus with a lighted destination approaching the bus stop, I sprinted across the parking lot like I was in a race against an invisible opponent. My skinny legs were spinning as I waved my arms and hollered to get the driver's attention.

Do you expect the driver to see a black person in the dark? The thought scared me. I had to catch that bus. My body reacted to fear, releasing a warm, gushing liquid between my legs. I kept on running, hoping it would stop flowing before I mounted the bus steps. It did. As I purchased my transfer to Ridgewood, I pretended not to feel my wet shoes and hoped there was no odor.

The only person on the bus was an old man with a stuffed, army duffle bag in his lap. He looked like he had nothing else to do but ride the bus all day long. It was ten after ten o'clock when the man's body odor overwhelmed me. As the last bus for the night headed downtown, I smiled from my back row seat. I had been worried about smelling like pee, but the old man had already stunk up the bus.

Rather than pout about Uncle Clyde's failure to pick me up, I sat on the bus staring out the window, thinking, "Thank you God for all the times when Uncle Clyde did come on time." I cringed at the thought of someone at Sears Town taking me home and then coming back to tell people I lived in a dump out in the woods. I thanked God for buses that shortened the distance I had to walk. That ride gave me time to rest my weary feet before walking the remaining miles home.

Being propelled by shame and consumed by guilt must have been the penalty for not revealing that I didn't have transportation. Getting to church some Sundays was also rough. People without a car have no business living way out in the country.

***

"Are you sure?" I asked the receptionist when I called Sears Roebuck and was told that I was scheduled to work from nine until noon on a Saturday morning. I was glad until I remembered that the bus doesn't come until nine. So, I had to get up extra early and walk to Ridgewood, six miles instead of three, to catch a bus. Passing the cemetery during the day, however, didn't bother me.

After work, I caught the one o'clock bus to Cashmere Road and was enjoying my stroll in the sunlight until the sky became cloudy and raindrops pelted the top of my head. I stood beneath a tree imagining the fun Gene Kelly had with his song, "I'm Singin' in the Rain." After getting drenched, I realized that it made more sense to keep on walking since I had no idea how long it would rain. My tennis shoes made a "squish, squish" sound as I hummed the song.

At one point I saw the sun shining through the rain and remembered Mama's saying that it was a sign that "the devil was beating his wife." I snickered at the thought of a woman being married to the devil. "What woman would want to live with a horned-creature wearing tight red pajamas and holding a pitchfork in his hand? What a stupid saying.

The rain stopped and a beautiful rainbow appeared. Then the August sun reappeared and dried my clothes and shoes before I got home.

"What happened to your hair?" Mama asked when she saw me.

"I got caught in the rain," I said.

"What rain? It didn't rain here."

"Doesn't my shriveled hair prove that it rained? I would never have left home with my hair like this. I'm just glad I got wet coming home rather than going to work. If it had been the other way around, I would have frightened all of our customers away."

***

I knew what to do the second time Uncle Clyde left me stranded at Sears. I caught the late-night bus as before, but decided not to disturb Naomi's parents again. I sang, as I ran down dark Cashmere Road.

When I approached the church cemetery, the Bible story about the crazy man who lived in the tombs came to mind. I thought I saw a shadow lurking behind a tombstone so I shot past the cemetery on foot faster than superman could fly.

My mama liked to say, "Watch the living, the dead can't hurt you." But I was thinking, "Living people hurt you, but dead people make you hurt yourself."

When I got a safe distance past the cemetery, I wondered which was more challenging, walking or hitching a ride with a crazy man. On, or off the job training. Getting a job, or keeping it. Staying safe at home and broke, or walking the streets at night with money. I had expected a job to solve my problems, not create new ones.

Chapter 19
FEELING INFERIOR

IN ELEVENTH GRADE I FELT like an invisible "kick me" sign was embedded on my forehead. The first blow came in homeroom when I opened a Manila envelope containing my progress report. Since I had all good grades and a high grade point average (GPA), I gasped when I saw a strange letter.

"What? A 'C' in Trigonometry!"

I blinked twice and then looked around homeroom class. Other students were poring over their report cards, too. I stared at the strange letter again. How did I get a 'C' when all my grades were B's and higher?

A flashback of the 'C' Mr. Glass had given all his students in my tenth grade Chemistry class came to mind. I had despised his grading system and his teaching style. But he did listen when I went to him privately, and he gave me the higher grade that I deserved. Teachers should know they cause students grief when they make mistakes.

Eager to point out the grading error, I marched straight over to Mrs. Honeywell's desk as soon as I entered her classroom.

"You made a mistake and gave me a 'C.' "

"A 'C' is not a bad grade," she said.

"But I never made less than a 'B' in this class."

"A 'C' is what you earned. You can work to improve it before the end of the marking period." She turned away, picked up a piece of chalk and wrote on the board.

"That's not my grade," I mumbled, feeling insulted. I shook my head and returned to my seat, angry. She wants me to listen to her but she won't listen to me.

I decided to find a way to get Mrs. Honeywell to

change my grade. She hadn't even said she'd check her math. What made her assume that I would be happy with a 'C?' Did she think she could cheat me just because she hadn't met my parents? Isn't a teacher supposed to base grades on the student's work?

During class that day and work that night, all I could think about was my teacher's disregard for my feelings. I had noticed how professional teachers could act when parents visit the classroom. Teachers respected students whose parents they knew. Convinced that Mrs. Honeywell would never have told my counselor's daughter, "A 'C' is good enough for you," I thought of ways to get Mama involved in my fight for a grade change.

After work that night, I burst into Mama's bedroom and found her working a newspaper crossword puzzle. I pushed my report card in front of her puzzle.

"Mrs. Honeywell didn't give me the grade I deserve. Mama, PLEASE come to my school tomorrow and talk to her. She won't listen to a student, but I know she'll listen to a parent."

"I don't know what to say to yo teacher," she said.

"You just show up at ten o'clock and I'll do all the talking."

Mama stared at my report card while I scribbled a note requesting a parent conference with Mrs. Honeywell. Then I handed her a Bic pen and she signed the paper without saying a word.

"Thank you," I said. "I'll see you at Madison tomorrow. Please ask Uncle Clyde to bring you on time."

I left Mama's room waving the note like a victory flag. My mama never visited schools because she liked to say, "Dem teachers don't need me gittin' in the way whilst they do their job." She said a parent should only show up when the child was in some kind of trouble. Well to me, a teacher cheating a child out of the right grade was trouble.

Before leaving home the next morning, I reminded Mama to be at school by ten o'clock. When I arrived, I delivered my signed note to the office secretary, and then went to first and second periods feeling confident that I'd be ready when it was time to speak up for myself.

In third period study hall, I sat staring at a book and praying that Mama would keep her word. Ten o'clock came and went. I felt disappointed. Seven minutes past the hour my heart fluttered when a boy tiptoed into study hall, whispered to the teacher, and then left. She looked at me and nodded toward the door.

"Goody! Mama came. Thank you God." I heaved a sigh of relief as I gathered my books.

Outside, the boy waiting to escort me said, "Your mother and father are in the counselor's office to talk to your teacher."

"Thanks." I smiled at him for assuming that Uncle Clyde was my daddy. I saw no need to correct him.

When I entered the room, Mr. Cannon, my counselor, was telling Mrs. Honeywell, Mama, and Uncle Clyde, "We like for parents to visit the school. They should be involved in their child's education." He saw me and then said, "Oh, Good morning, Davida."

"Good morning everybody," I said.

My shy mama looked like she was on the verge of melting in her leather seat. "This is my mother and her brother, Uncle Clyde. I told my mama about the low grade I received on my report card in Trigonometry. Mrs. Honeywell gave me the wrong grade and I can prove it."

I opened my notebook to the papers behind the yellow divider labeled Trigonometry and flipped through each graded assignment, holding up page after page so everyone in the room could clearly see the big, red colored pencil grade of 'A' or 'B.' When I finished I said, "I keep all my work until the end of the semester or even until the end of the school year to study for tests."

"Let me see your notebook?" Mrs. Honeywell said.

I handed it to her.

She flipped through each page. Then she opened her roll book and ran her finger down and across to the last column. "You're right. I made a mistake. I looked at the wrong line. You earned a 'B+.' I'm sorry. I will correct your report card."

"Thank you," I said, smiling, as I stared at Mama.

"I thank you too," Mama said. "That 'C' was really bothering Davida."

Uncle Clyde laughed and said, "Well now she won't hafta worry 'bout it no mo."

"I thank all of you for helping to clear up this matter," Mr. Cannon said. "If there's nothing else, then we can let Mrs. Honeywell return to her post. Agreed?"

"Yessir." I nodded agreement.

"I thank both of ya'll," Mama said, getting up to leave. Dressed in her green frock and black sweater, she looked cute on her first visit to my school. I was proud of her for coming and of myself for defending my grade. Just because we were poor didn't mean people could mistreat us.

On our way to the exit, the taps on Uncle Clyde's big heels clicked loudly as they connected with the waxed wooden floor. I was proud of him, too, for coming inside dressed in his mechanic's uniform.

"Thank you so much for coming," I said, stopping to hug Mama at the door.

"It's been a long time since I been to school," she said, giggling. "Things shold done changed from that one room schoolhouse I went to in seventh grade."

"Now you see how much power parents have these days," I said.

Without saying a word, she went out the door that Uncle Clyde held open for her.

I returned to study hall feeling victorious, yet sad, because Mrs. Honeywell had refused to listen to me when I first told her my grade was wrong. She had to know that everybody makes mistakes sometimes. Just in case she was upset with me for reporting her mistake to the counselor, I was determined to study harder to be sure I never made a 'C' on any of my assignments in Trigonometry.

The second blow came that afternoon. I was in the physical education locker room stepping into my blue gym suit when two girls approached my bench.

"Rumor has it that you challenged a teacher," Roberta said.

"That's none of your business," I said.

"Mrs. Honeywell said one of her students upset her so much she couldn't teach this morning," Johnnie Mae said. "Who do you think you are to criticize a teacher?"

"I told you it's none of your business," I said, pushing my locker shut.

"You ought to be ashamed of yourself!" Roberta yelled.

Knowing they were trying to pick a fight, I headed toward the gym. Even if they called me a coward, I was not about to let them mess up my good citizenship.

"Look at her skinny scarred-up legs. Mosquitoes must love her!" Johnnie Mae said.

"I would never dress for PE if I had insect bites on my legs like that!" Roberta hollered, loud enough for all the girls in the locker room to hear.

"Even boys have prettier legs than that ugly duckling," Johnny Mae chimed in.

Walking ahead of those loudmouths into the gymnasium, I was more upset about the rumor that I had confronted a teacher than the insults about my legs. I detested people who spread lies, but those girls weren't going to get the truth from me. What happened was none of their business.

Angry glares from a few classmates made me feel like I had leprosy. I botched my gymnastics exercises. PE couldn't end soon enough. That day I didn't complete one cartwheel. I think I tried too hard.

Showering after class, I dreaded having my body open to inspection like I was a hunk of meat in a butcher shop. Who decided that school locker rooms shouldn't have shower curtains? I anticipated more insults from the lionesses, but heard nothing.

Self-conscious feelings about my visible defects made me pay attention to things I'd never noticed before. Students my age had no shame as they strutted around in the nude. How could they be so bold? Three skinny girls bragged about advancing from an "A" bra cup size to a "B" and even to a "C." They were telling all their business. The Jergens lotion that I had considered top of the line seemed cheap in comparison to the scented lotion in cute containers other girls smeared on their skin. Some wore pretty laced underwear and shiny colored panties with a matching bra. Still others sprayed on Estee Lauder and other perfumes that I thought were for women only. I'd never thought of myself as a woman—just Mama's helper.

Where had I been all this time? For too long I'd hidden behind narrow locker doors so no one would notice me putting on my plain, white cotton underwear or rubbing Blue Seal Vaseline Petroleum Jelly on my ashy skin. I'd never noticed what was happening around me before, and now I felt embarrassed.

Did I really need to take physical education? No. I got plenty of exercise walking to Sears Town and working at home. I dressed and hurried out of the locker room wondering how I could get out of taking PE without getting a bad grade.

The next morning while riding the school bus, thoughts of the incident with Mrs. Honeywell reminded me that parents have power to change situations. So, I scribbled a note from Mama that read: *Please exempt my child, Davida Kincaid, from dressing for PE due to a medical problem.*

I nudged sleepy-eyed Rosa Lee who was seated beside me.

"Hey, wake up and sign my mama's name for me."

"What?" she said, sitting up.

"Here." I stuck my ballpoint pen in her hand and put the note in front of her. "Scribble Blossom Kincaid with your left hand. Sign it real fast so nobody can read your writing."

She signed it without even reading the note, handed me my pen and then closed her eyes again. I tucked the note in a secure spot inside my pleather pocketbook.

I leaned back in my seat and thought about high school being a place of torment for poor students. Some classmates bragged about their Pierre Cardin fashions and Gucci shoes. None of them lived in the country. Some could only dream of owning one mohair sweater while others had a different one for Monday through Friday. Pretending not to envy those whose parents had money was a challenge. At least I didn't have to wear the same outfit day after day like a girl in my homeroom class who dressed in a long-sleeved tan dress and white cotton stockings. I would never think of stealing anything, but I could understand why students' clothes sometimes walked away from the PE lockers.

When we arrived at Madison, I went straight to the office, presented my forged note to the secretary, and received a printed PE exemption slip. How easy! She asked no questions about my medical problem or even seemed sorry to hear about it. That was good. I hadn't decided which illness I'd say was causing me a problem, so she saved me from telling a lie.

A week later, Mr. Smith, my homeroom teacher, read the following memorandum to the class: "Due to a rash of requests for exemption from PE, all future requests must state the specific medical condition and be signed by a physician as well as your parent."

"The office got wind of your tricks," he told the class. "Hint, hint."

I got my exemption in the nick of time. Then it occurred to me that I could have started the epidemic. Telling that lie made me feel guilty and scared I'd get sick for real, even though God knew I needed to stay out of the locker room before I got in trouble.

The door opened and a slender, new boy entered homeroom. Mr. Smith assigned him the empty seat between Gerald, the football player who rode my school bus, and me.

"Do you play football?" Gerald said.

"I like the sport, but it doesn't like me," Horace said. "I have hemophilia."

"Hemo-phi-lia?" Gerald said. "What's that?"

"A hemophiliac bleeds longer than most people. When we get injured, the blood takes longer to clot and we could bleed to death. So I can't afford to do any activity where I might get hurt, and that includes PE exercises."

I squirmed in my seat, wanting to kick myself for lying about having a medical condition. Horace had a valid reason to be exempted from PE, but I didn't. He wanted to participate, but he couldn't. He was brave enough to tell a stranger the truth about a problem over which he had no control. I admired his positive self-image, but mine needed a boost. He knew his limitations and accepted them. Why couldn't I do the same without shame?

Chapter 20

NO COMPROMISE
ON PROM NIGHT

TOWARD THE END OF ELEVENTH GRADE, my inferiority complex prompted me to make a big blunder. Wanting to look and feel special at Madison High's junior-senior prom, I sent a letter from South Carolina to my sister Lynette in New York requesting a beautiful, one-of-a-kind gown that would make me the belle of the ball.

Two weeks later I tore open a package from Lynette and pulled out a royal blue floor-length, sleeveless dress. To my surprise, the box also included silver gloves that covered my elbows, a tiara that made me look like a queen, and satin silver pumps and a matching clutch. Nobody would expect me to show up looking eye-popping gorgeous. I giggled at the thought.

The rule for the junior-senior prom was "No Date, No Admittance." Confident that I would go, I paid my fees knowing that I had everything for the occasion, except a date.

A teacher, Mrs. Davis, was responsible for playing matchmaker for students who had not chosen their own prom date. And a few days prior to the big event, she called me into her classroom.

"I matched you with Theodore because he also lives on Cashmere Road," she said.

"Theodore! He's a goofball."

"Well, goofball or not, he's the most logical choice," she said. "He has already consented to be your date. Either accept him, or you can't attend."

Disappointed, I thought for a moment then heard myself say, "Oh well, Theodore it is."

"Good!" she said. "It's only for a few hours for one night. You'll get along just fine."

I left her classroom with Theodore on my mind. He lived in a big, new brick house on Cashmere Road. His family drove a white Lincoln Continental. He was tall and slender and had a gap between his two front teeth. That's all I knew about him. I couldn't imagine spending a whole evening with a boy I really didn't know, but I was glad he had been brave enough to accept me as his date without knowing much about me.

***

The evening of the prom, while anticipating Theodore's arrival in his parents' luxury car, I went out on my front porch to check the temperature. What a perfect evening in May. Admiring the full moon above thousands of pine trees, I pretended that the sound of chirping crickets was a musical interlude that would continue to play while he pinned a lovely corsage on my dress. I pranced back and forth practicing ways to show off the shiny, silver pumps beneath my gown. He was going to see a beautiful lady who was all decked out from head to toe. Feeling quite pleased with myself, I went back inside to wait for the right moment to step out and dazzle my date.

At six-thirty, the time Theodore had promised to pick me up, a yellow Mustang that needed a muffler rattled into our dirt driveway. The car made enough noise to wake up the dead. I went to the door.

"What the...?" A Mustang! I gaped at the sight of Theodore getting out of the car. Grabbing my silver clutch, I hurried outside to avoid inviting him into my tiny blockhouse. My six little sisters crowded the front door but stayed inside because I'd dared them to come outside.

Strutting across the yard, Theodore looked like a proud penguin dressed in a black tuxedo and white shirt decorated with a black bow tie. Both his hands were empty. Already annoyed because of the noisy car and no corsage, I had a feeling it was going to be a challenging night. Hadn't he heard the instructions Mrs. Davis gave us?

"You look beautiful," he said, stepping onto the porch.

"Thank you," I said. "You look nice, too. Stand still and let me pin this boutonniere on the buttonhole of your lapel like Mrs. Davis told us." He stood motionless while I inserted the tiny flower. Maybe he left my corsage in the car. Stay calm, Davida.

"Blunder number one from the goofball," I thought.

"Ouch!" I pricked my finger on my first attempt to pin the flower. Mrs. Davis had warned us not to put on our gloves until after the pinning, just in case we got a bloody prick. She'd thought of everything we needed to know. I tried again and the boutonniere stayed in place.

"There," I said. "It looks perfect!"

"Then let's go," he said. "My older brother Thaddeus is our chauffeur tonight."

"Ooooh," I said, thinking, that was a clever idea.

"Let me escort you like I'm supposed to," he said. He bent his arm and I gently grabbed hold.

Be nice, Davida. He's trying to be a gentleman just like the teacher said.

Theodore opened the door on the passenger side and pulled up the seat so I could climb in the back of the two-door car.

"Hi," I grunted to his brother as I plopped down.

"Would you move on over?" Theodore said.

Surprised that he didn't plan to walk around to the other side, I slid behind the driver. He acted like Thaddeus was a real chauffeur.

Theodore must have detected my negative attitude because he quickly said, "Oh, I left your corsage at home in the refrigerator."

"That's nice to know," I said.

A few minutes later, Thaddeus pulled into their paved driveway and parked next to the Lincoln. Without saying a word he got out, left the driver's door open, and went into the house.

"Some chauffeur!" Theodore mumbled. Then he pushed the front seat forward, opened the passenger door and climbed out. I sat wondering what was going on until he showed up on the driver's side and pushed that seat forward.

"Come on inside and meet my parents," he said.

"I can wait in the car while you go get the corsage," I said.

"No, I want you to come inside. My mother wants to see your dress."

"Oh, all right." He took my arm as I climbed out of the car, and then escorted me through the side door. We walked through the kitchen and entered a huge living room with all white furnishings.

"Surprise!" His mother shouted. We looked in her direction and were greeted with the flash from a Polaroid Land Camera. His father and Thaddeus stood grinning as his mother clicked about ten shots of us.

"Wait!" Theodore hollered. He ran to the refrigerator and returned carrying a clear container with a white flower that I'd never seen before. Printed on the package was the name Orchid. Though disappointed that he didn't get a carnation or a rose like Mrs. Davis had recommended, I was glad that he had remembered the corsage.

Standing still like a model posing for a portrait, I waited forever for Theodore to pin the corsage in place. After a few unsuccessful attempts, I hoped I wouldn't have to yell at him for sticking me with that long pin. Although I was anxious about getting to the Masonic Temple before the doors closed, I pretended to be patient. His family didn't seem worried about the time. They watched him struggle and laughed each time the flower drooped when he removed his hand.

His mother took pictures of every move her son made. Near seven o'clock she said, "Please allow me to do it."

My nerves stopped standing at attention and relaxed

when Theodore sighed, stepped aside and handed her the corsage and the pin. She finished the job with one stick and then leaned back, stared into my eyes and smiled.

"You look simply beautiful," she said. "My son has great taste."

Flashes from the camera blinded me as Thaddeus took several shots of his mother standing with me. Theodore and I posed for additional pictures with his father, mother and brother in their beautiful living room. Feeling better with my corsage in place, I smiled and thoroughly enjoyed all the praises lavished upon me. Why couldn't my family be like this one?

"We've got to go now," Thaddeus said, staring at his watch.

"Here," his father said, handing him some keys. "Drive the Lincoln."

I couldn't stop smiling as we headed for the car. Nobody knew how happy I was not to ride in a noisy Mustang to the classy prom.

Thaddeus sat behind the steering wheel while Theodore opened the rear door. The white leather interior invited me to sink down in the cushiony seat, so I got in and made myself comfortable beside the window. This time my date closed the door and then walked around to the other side. I felt a bit uncomfortable when he slid to the middle of the roomy backseat, but relaxed when he started talking to his brother.

"We're off to the prom," Thaddeus said, putting on a cap with a bib. "Lady and gent, I'm at your service."

Theodore and Thaddeus joked about their mother's photo shoot and how her excitement had rubbed off on their father. Once in a while I chimed in, but mostly, I listened to them.

"This is a first," Thaddeus said. "Pops never ever trusted me behind the wheel in this car unless he was in the passenger seat."

"Yeah," Theodore said, "I've never seen Moms and Pops so excited. They had more fun helping me get ready than I did. I almost thought they were coming, too."

Perhaps he's not such a goofball after all. He's just comical. I was pleasantly surprised to learn that I'd misjudged him.

As we entered the prom, I was overwhelmed by the Hawaiian decorations hanging from the ceiling and the walls.

"This place looks spectacular!" I said.

"Yeah," Theodore said, "This is great!"

Handsome gents dressed in tuxedoes made a lie out of the expression, "Clothes don't make the man." Even the most obnoxious boys conducted themselves like sophisticated gentlemen.

Dolled up girls flaunting long gowns glided all over the room like they were in a beauty pageant. Who said, "Too much powder and paint can't make you what you ain't?" Not true. I didn't recognize some classmates I'd known for years.

Mine was the only royal blue gown. A few beauties also flaunted a tiara, but only two others had orchids pinned to their dress. My silver gloves and slippers made me a rare southern belle indeed.

A boy seated at a table near the dance floor waved at Theodore while we were standing around absorbing the beautiful setting. "Green Onions" by Booker T & the MGs played in the background when my date escorted me to a seat next to his friend.

"Man, I'm surprised to see the two of you together," the boy said.

"Keep on living and you're bound to encounter other surprises," Theodore said.

Good answer. Theodore was gaining my respect. I appreciated him for not saying that Mrs. Davis matched us. That was our business.

To my surprise he was a good dancer. I kept him busy on the floor most of the night so we wouldn't have to try talking over loud music. Once or twice we sat through a song that neither of us liked. We spent that time nibbling on snacks and talking with another couple at our table.

When it was time for couples to take keepsake prom pictures, Theodore whispered, "Will you pay for a picture of the two of us together?"

"What? Of course not," I snapped, feeling insulted. "A boy is supposed to have money on a date."

I got up quickly and left the table while Theodore scrambled to pull out my chair. Reluctantly, I paid the five-dollar sitting fee for a single person and then glanced over at Theodore as I waited in line. He was standing along the roped off area looking dejected as he watched all the other happy couples pose for pictures by a professional photographer. I was angry with him for not having any money and I felt deceived by his parents for sending their son to the prom with empty pockets.

"What's wrong?" Theodore asked when I finally returned to our table. I'd deliberately avoided him by allowing couples to jump in line ahead of me.

"Nothing," I lied.

Just then the deejay announced, "And now it's time for the last dance of the evening. Grab that prom date because Ben E. King and the Drifters are coming up next with 'Save the Last Dance For Me.' Get ready. Get set. One, two, three! Everybody dance!"

"Let's dance," Theodore said, standing up.

"My feet hurt after all that standing in line," I said, without looking at him. I sat down and he pushed my chair beneath me. I was sulking over spending my own money.

He sat back down. We both watched all the other couples dance together.

What a bummer. While I'm making him miserable, I'm spoiling my own fun. "I'm ready to go whenever you are," I said, before the last dance ended.

"Okay. We can head out now. Thaddeus is waiting for us."

On the ride home, we sat on opposite ends of the long back seat. Neither of us said a word, but I had lots of things on my mind. Why had I ended up with a date that had no money? He had a whole year to save for this special night. Lots of students planned to go somewhere else afterwards, but we couldn't. Didn't he know he'd need money at the prom? I didn't know, but I brought some just in case. I'm sure I hurt his feelings, but he deserved to suffer for hurting mine.

I wondered what he'd tell his family about our date and started feeling sorry for my behavior. There was no way I could change what had already happened at the prom. Why had I acted mean at picture time? Everything up to that point had been great. How could I have hurt his feelings after his family had treated me so special?

Thaddeus must have detected the arctic blast in the backseat because he popped in an eight-track cartridge and began singing "The Tracks of My Tears" with Smokey Robinson and the Miracles. I stared at the darkness wishing we could relive the last half of our evening.

When we reached my house, Theodore came around and opened the back door for me and walked me to my front door. Without saying a word, he reached for my gloved hand, raised it to his lips and kissed it.

"Thank you for going to the prom with me," he said.

"Thank you for taking me," I said. "Good night." I went inside as he stood watching.

"Good night," he said, as I closed the door.

***

Rather than apologize for being selfish, I avoided Theodore for the remaining five weeks of school. The prom was the only thing that we had to talk about and it was over.

One week after we ended our eleventh grade year, Theodore died. I heard the announcement on radio station WOIC and called Elaine. She'd heard the news, too, so we agreed to attend his service together.

At his funeral, I gasped when I saw a prom picture taken by his mother on the cover of the obituary. A separate page contained other photographs from that night. Poor woman. She would have been delighted to see a picture of her son actually at the prom, but I didn't let it happen.

Theodore's father stood in front of the microphone, opened his mouth and wept. Hearing him cry was a tearjerker for the rest of us. Loud sobbing was heard all over the church until his mother went and stood beside her husband. She put a white handkerchief in his hand and he wiped his eyes. Then she placed her hand on his arm.

"What a beautiful couple, even though they're hurting," I thought.

He sniffed and then spoke to the congregation.

"The doctors told my wife and me that we could lose our son at any time. Theo was twelve when they discovered he had a rare blood disease. But we never told him. That would have killed him. We just let him go on enjoying his life as long as he could."

He stopped talking.

His wife leaned over, held up a prom picture, and spoke into the mic. "Attending the prom was the highlight of Theodore's life," she said. "He was so happy and looked so handsome that night. My son was so excited that he left home without his wallet. It was a good thing he wasn't driving."

People laughed, but I choked. Her words pricked my heart like needles being pushed in a pincushion. I felt like a killer. Maybe I'd stabbed him to death by chiding him for not having any money that night. How could I have known he'd forgotten his wallet?

After the funeral, I stood on the church grounds and wept.

My best friend, Elaine, came over and put her arms around me.

"Tell me what you've been holding back," she said. "Get it off your chest. You're crying like you lost your best friend and I know you weren't that close to him."

"I feel so bad about Theodore," I said. "I feel like it's my fault he died. I behaved badly toward him on prom night. I wish I could have found it in my heart to ask him to forgive me. But I was too proud to admit I was wrong. Now it's too late."

"You didn't kill him," she said.

"But he was a good person and I wouldn't let him forget his one mistake. I acted like a genuine brat on prom night. Now I hate that I'll never be able to ask him to forgive me."

"Yeah, that awful." When she paused for a minute, I knew something profound was about to roll off her lips. "Would you rather be the one who died?"

"What made you ask that?" I stared into her eyes wondering how she could joke about something so serious.

"Because you have to learn to forget the things you can't change," she said. "He's dead now and you can't change it. You'll make some more mistakes as long as you're alive. Just try to do better next time."

"But why did he have to die so young?"

"Didn't your sister Zenobia die young too? Look around you in this cemetery. Don't you see graves of all sizes out here?"

"I know. I know. But maybe our senior year I could have told him why I got so upset with him. I needed time to figure out why I felt disrespected. So many scars had already bruised my ego. He didn't tell me he had forgotten his wallet. I made a big deal out of his mistake and spoiled my own fun. From now on I'm going to apologize and ask forgiveness while I have the chance."

"Good for you! You got anything you need to ask me to forgive you for?"

"I can't think of anything right now," I said, laughing as I scratched my head.

It felt good to dump all the garbage I'd carried inside. Elaine had helped me just by listening. She had a knack for getting me to look at myself, or a situation, differently. She was right. I would make more mistakes in this life. So, instead of beating myself up over things I could not change, I decided to learn the art of compromise.

Chapter 21
MY FIRST BOYFRIEND

ELEVEN YEARS OF SCHOOL! FOR WHAT? I closed my eyes as our school bus drove past Theodore's house on the first day of twelfth grade. He had come so close to being a senior. Why God? Why did he die so young? Did he ever have a girlfriend? Did he know how to kiss? Did he ever have sex? It must be awful to die when you've never really lived. Life doesn't really start until after graduation. No wonder his father never told him he had a disease.

My tears made pine trees droop like candles dripping wax. Sniffling, I leaned my head against the window.

A tap on the shoulder startled me. After wiping both eyes with my fingertips, I turned toward Rosa Lee, my best friend at school and bus seatmate.

"A penny for your thoughts," she said.

"Ohhh… seeing Theodore's house brought back so many memories."

"Yeah. I thought that's why you were crying. Death doesn't care who it attacks. A loss is a loss and it doesn't matter if you're a girlfriend or wife or sister or mother or only a prom date."

"I know. Thanks for understanding."

I turned back toward the window and closed my eyes to blot out thoughts of me acting like a selfish brat on prom night. When death took Theodore, it destroyed all hope of him forgiving me. Who knew that a dead person could control the living? Dang! Relationships are hard work. They always require compromise. A guilty conscience makes a hard pillow.

Senior year was off to a rough start. "I can, I will, I must succeed," I mumbled. That was the mantra I'd made up in tenth grade at the time I decided to become the first person in my family to graduate from high school, go to college, get a good job, and help Mama move to a nice house. It encouraged me whenever things got tough. During my last year of school, nothing, especially not senioritis, would hinder me from walking across the stage to get my diploma. I never thought about death and I hope it never thought about me.

Could I have felt any worse if Theodore had been my boyfriend? His parents got along fine the two times I saw them together. But my big blunder with their son taught me to insist that my husband and I make up if we have a disagreement. It would hurt me too much not to be able to apologize if something bad happened to him.

Am I selfish, or crazy, to keep hoping Mama and Daddy will get back together? They could if they wanted to because separated, but not divorced, means they are still married. Oh how I'd love for them to feel guilty for breaking up our family.

Suddenly, I thought of O. C. Smith's song "Hickory Holler's Tramp." My situation couldn't be unique if he sang about children with different daddies and how awful life could be when a father runs off and leaves his poor family behind. His song proved that he could relate to how I was feeling. I fought hard to keep from sniffling again.

That won't be my story. I'm going to marry a man who loves his family. We'll have three children that all look like my husband and me. After we become gray-haired grandparents, walk with a cane, wear a hearing aid or dentures, then it will be okay to die. But before I get a husband, I need to figure out how a girl gets a boyfriend.

When the bus arrived at Madison High, underclassmen let seniors exit first. I proudly got off behind skinny Rosa Lee who stood six feet two inches tall. Her height intimidated anyone that might look at her cross-eyed. I was skinny too, and only five feet five inches but still considered one of the tallest girls on the bus. As the classmates I'd known since elementary school got off the bus, they looked like grown men sporting mustaches and women with big breasts and broad hips. Gosh! We'd all gone through a lot of changes over the years.

Rosa Lee and I talked as we walked side by side toward the building. I liked the way she spoke her mind and was bold enough to butcher grammar by using "doesn't" in every sentence. For years she'd trusted me enough to give me a credit account at her father's grocery store on Cashmere Road. Today she helped me to take my mind off Theodore by saying, "Girl, he's too busy having a good time in heaven to think about you. So forget about him."

Neither of us had found a boyfriend yet. Rosa Lee wanted a guy who was taller, because both her mama and daddy were tall. We agreed that tall boys were made for tall girls even though they mostly chose short girls.

I didn't tell Rosa Lee that I had a crush on a tall boy named Billy Summer because he might be the one for her. I didn't know how to get his attention, so I decided if he ever noticed me, fine. If not, I'd just focus on graduation and plan to meet my husband in college. But, should I wait until then or get a boyfriend now so I'll know how to act next year? Boys can be slow to notice when a girl likes them.

A few days after school started, Rosa Lee and I were eating lunch in the cafeteria when she pulled a note out of her skirt pocket and handed it to me.

Ronnie, the class clown, who was almost six feet, had scribbled, "I like you. Tall girls are so attractuv to me." "He likes you!" I said. "So what if he doesn't know how to spell attractive. Do you like him?"

"Well, sorta, I guess. But he doesn't meet my height requirements."

"He's almost as tall as you," I said.

"But not quite. I doesn't want a man I have to look down to."

While we talked about why she might want to get to know Ronnie better, I wondered what I wanted in a boyfriend. Why did I like Billy Summer's cool walk and thick, juicy black lips. For some reason, I thought he was cute. What features did I have that a boy might find attractive?

"Girl, I'm going to tell anybody I know with a problem to call you. I doesn't want to hear their stuff but you listen real good."

"That's fine," I said, handing back her note.

Rosa Lee's cousin called me that same night. I listened as she shared personal business. After that, other girls started dumping garbage about the opposite sex. I encouraged them to look at the other person's point of view and offered a different way to process each experience.

Most girlfriends had felt pressured into having sex to keep a guy. In each case the boys begged until they got what they wanted. Rather than keep the girl they scored a touchdown with, many of the boys moved on to someone else. If the girl got pregnant, then most of the time he had to marry her. That's when he made her life miserable. I never took sides or violated their confidence so before long I got the nickname "Class shrink."

"Now I understand why Mama said, "Keep your pants up and your dress down," I told Elaine, my shrink. "But I still wish I knew what it was like to have my own boyfriend."

"You just wait. Love comes naturally. You can't make a man love you," she said.

One morning I stared out the school bus window, thinking, "Okay, God, how is it that I listen to other girls talk about their boyfriend but I don't have one. I've got feelings, too, you know."

In Social Studies class we learned about cliques— small groups of people who spend time with like-minded folks and snub outsiders. At first, the teacher seemed to be talking about discrimination between whites and Negroes. But then I realized that Madison High had a serious case of city versus country students, bright versus dull, well-off versus poor. Although I got along with almost everybody, cliques at school were part of the reason for my decision to stay away from people like the girls that had insulted me last year in the locker room.

Life was so much simpler when we were little and everybody played together. Boys and girls were all friends. The older we became the farther we grew apart. Losing friendships is almost as hard, or harder, than losing someone who dies. A living person might choose to dump you for someone else.

Where does a girl meet a boy? My job left me with little time to socialize after school. We spent plenty of time riding to school every morning, but the boys on my bus were boring. Besides singing Hambone, they mostly talked about stuff like sports, bulls hopping the fence, butchering hogs, and cars they dreamed of owning one day. Must a girl be interested in sports, sex, violence, or cars to attract a guy?

Rosa Lee and I discussed the lesson on cliques during lunch.

"You doesn't need to hang out with me," she said. "You ought to get in a clique with your intelligent classmates who read all the time like you."

"No, I don't fit in that crowd." I thought about people that act snooty because they wear nice outfits, live in big brick homes and have two parents who give them an allowance and set a curfew. "I can't even attend the football games because they're always at night when I either work or have to worry about getting home. I guess I'm just bored with my life right now."

"Me too," she said. "I reckon we're both in the same boat. We live too far out in the country to hang out with city folk who doesn't know a hatchet from a hammer."

"I wish I didn't know the difference between them," I said.

"They probably doesn't know how good they've got it," she giggled.

"Girl, you'd get an 'F' in English if the teacher knew how you use 'doesn't' all the time," I said, giggling.

"Well, doesn't everybody have a favorite word?

Doesn't you like to say 'dang!'? Doesn't students say four-letter cuss words when parents ain't around? Doesn't I have the right to talk any way I want to outside the classroom?"

"That's enough! I must admit I like hearing you say that word. You sound so proper and so wrong. Correcting you is a waste of breath, like blowing a bubble that pops before it goes anywhere."

"We both know students who use profanity when grownups doesn't hear them. One incorrect verb ain't all that bad."

"Okay. Keep on saying your doesn'ts."

"Hey, I been watching you for a long time, and I likes what I see," a man's deep voice interrupted.

I looked up from my tray and saw, James Pitchford, a 6-foot-4 basketball player nicknamed "Slinky" because he liked to bend and sway on the court.

"Do you mind if I call you Dimples." He flashed his big white pearls at me.

I smiled back.

"See, that's what I like. Your dimples are so cute," he said, straddling his long legs over the bench seat in front of me, and not Rosa Lee.

Instantly, I changed my mind about tall boys being made for tall girls and short boys for short girls. Hmmm...who cares about height when they're attracted to somebody?

James had a wooden toothpick protruding out of his mouth that bounced up and down between his thick lips. I expected him to swallow it at any moment.
"Flattery will get you nowhere," I said.

Rosa Lee continued eating and pretended to ignore our conversation.

James talked a lot about nothing in particular while I ate and listened.

"I heard you're a good listener," he said. "They got you pegged right."

"Sounds like a good fit," Rosa Lee muttered. "A talker

and a listener." She took her tray and left me talking to James when the bell sounded.

"I'm a slow eater," I said, picking up my tray and heading for the drop off counter. "Sorry. I've got to run."

"Tomorrow, same time and place?" he said.

"Tomorrow," I giggled.

Outside the cafeteria, James and I headed in opposite directions to get to our next class.

My dimples attracted him. Dimples! I'd never even paid much attention to them.

The next day, James came over and slid beside me on the cafeteria bench. He complained about the food while I ate meatloaf, corn and mashed potatoes. There was no way I'd let him spoil my one good meal for the day. I listened as he talked about basketball and how much girls like athletes. He sounded egotistical. Had God sent him in answer to my prayer?

"Davida is it all right if I call you tonight?" he said.

"Okay."

"Then I need your phone number." He pushed a notepad beside my tray and handed me a ballpoint pen. He talked while I jotted down my number.

"I tried to get the number from your girl, Rosa Lee, but she said nobody calls you without your okay. Your friend protects you. I likes that."

"That's my friend. Call after ten. I have to work tonight."

"Gotcha," he said.

After Uncle Clyde dropped me off at home that night, James called at ten o'clock sharp. I picked up the receiver as soon as I heard the fourth long ring on our eight party line. We talked so long that he dozed off and snored.

"James!" I said, and he woke up. We laughed and talked some more until I dozed off.

"Davida!" He said and I woke up. That's when a lady in the background yelled, "Hang up that phone and go to sleep."

"See you tomorrow at lunch," he said, and then I heard the dial tone.

On the way to school the next morning, I told Rosa Lee about our long phone conversation.

"Watch out for that guy," she said. "He doesn't know I heard he's a jerk."

"You mean a jock," I giggled.

"You doesn't know him. He's a jock and a jerk."

I felt like she was jealous because he was tall enough to be her boyfriend but he had chosen me.

"Okay, we'll see what happens," I said.

James sat with us and talked during lunch. Rosa Lee and I listened, but she had nothing to say. After she finished eating and left, James told me why he'd hung up so fast.

"My mama had said ten o'clock is too late to talk on the phone. So I held the receiver in the bed underneath the covers to muffle my voice. I forgot where I was when I yelled your name. I knew I was in trouble when I heard my bedroom door open. My mama can hear bird poop drop on the roof. Next time I'll call around eight. I likes hearing your voice. I could listen to you all night."

I smiled to show off my dimples. He didn't realize that sweet talk wasn't going to make me go crazy over him. I'd heard too much and seen too many pregnant girls stand up in church confessing they had sinned.

For almost three weeks James and I had a laughing good time eating lunch together and talking on the phone at night. He called me "his girl" and gave me one of his basketball pictures so I could keep him close to my heart. Most of the time Rosa Lee would eat with us and then leave because she didn't like James. But I liked him and that's all that mattered. I was learning how to be a girlfriend.

On the day of James's first basketball game of the season, I was standing outside Madison High that morning selling Y-Teen potato chips when a girl wearing a cheerleader's uniform approached me. I held out a bag of chips and said, "Twenty-five cents."

She shook her head, no. "Do you know James Pitchford?"

"Who wants to know?" I said.

"Oh, my name is Katie. I'm a tenth grader. So do you know him?"

"Yes."

"Do you have a picture of him?"

"Yeah, why are you asking me?"

"Because he said he gave you his last basketball picture. I just want to see if he really was on the team."

Proud of my boyfriend, I opened my billfold and showed her James's eleventh grade school picture in which he balanced a ball on the tip of his index finger and wore jersey number twenty-seven.

"Oh, so he was on the team!" She sounded pleasantly surprised. "He told me you two were talking."

"And?"

"Oh, that's all. I just wanted to see the picture." Then she left and joined two other cheerleaders who had stood at a distance. They walked away together.

Thinking it odd that he had talked to a tenth grader about us, that night on the phone I told him about the strange conversation.

"A girl named Katie asked me about you today."

"What did she want?" he said.

"She asked to see your picture?"

"Did you show it to her?"

"Yeah. Wasn't that what you wanted me to do? "

"Why did you show her my picture?" he yelled.

"She wouldn't have known I had it if you hadn't told her."

"Couldn't you tell she wanted to cause trouble between us?"

"No, I couldn't. I thought that you and I were tight. The tone of your voice proves you're not as slick as you think you are. You should be angry with yourself for telling her about the picture you gave me."

"I see you don't think I'm worth fighting for," he said.

"Fight over you! Boy, give me a break!" I slammed the receiver down in the cradle.

How was I supposed to know that I couldn't trust him to only want me for his girlfriend? I was angry with James and angry with myself. How was I supposed to know that Katie was trouble? He was my first boyfriend. Why would he tell her that I had his picture if he hadn't wanted her to see it? Boys!

I'd hoped James would call back and apologize. But he didn't. So, I cried myself to sleep. I didn't understand what had happened to us. We were just getting to know each other. On the phone, he had even said he loved me. Can love be turned on and off like a faucet?

The next day James was seated beside Katie when I entered the cafeteria.

"That James doesn't waste any time moving on to the next girl," Rosa Lee said.

I pretended not to notice them or hear her. Oh well! It was nice while it lasted. He didn't call back because he wanted us to breakup and blame me. Boys like to blame girls the same way Adam blamed Eve from the beginning.

"When he doesn't score with one he goes chasing another skirt," Rosa Lee said.

"Really?" It felt good having a friend who knew me well enough to know that I hadn't given up my virginity to keep a boyfriend. "Well, Katie taught me that some people have ulterior motives for getting in your business."

"You got that right," she said.

"Genuine friendships are rare. If you don't believe me, watch what happens when you're having a bad day."

"I doesn't get what you mean."

"Well, when someone asks, 'How are you?' they expect to hear, 'Fine.' If you say how you really feel, you'll end up talking to the wind because that person will be gone."

"You're right. It doesn't pay to tell the truth," she said.

I sat in the cafeteria eating and thinking how, over-night, James acted like he'd forgotten all about me. Occasionally, I glanced over at him and felt my heart go pitter-patter. He was talking with a toothpick between his lips and I pictured him saying, "Hey, I been watching you for a long time and I likes what I see." I fell for that line. So, why should he change it? Maybe he's telling her he likes the big calves in her legs or her flat rump. At least now I know that my dimples are attractive.

Had he staged the break up with me so he could say it was my fault? I'm sure he liked the fact that she was bold enough to come up in my face to ask me about my boyfriend. And she did in front of witnesses. I never would have done anything like that.

Should I have been more excited about going with a basketball player? Maybe it's a good thing he moved on to find his match. He and his cheerleader friend can go to games together.

I stared at my tray wondering why James didn't tell me he'd found somebody he liked better. Doesn't he know it's easier to tell the truth than to conceal a lie? Does the dumper feel guilty? Or is that emotion reserved for the dumpee? Daddy didn't seem to feel guilty for dumping Mama for Miss Annie Mae. Do men have a heart? Did James ever really like me? How does a girl know if a boy is the right one for her? Dang! I was full of questions.

As James and Katie left the cafeteria together, I thought about Daddy going to be with Miss Annie Mae. I never asked Mama how she felt about that. I knew I'd feel much worse if I had been married to James or we had been together for a long time. Pregnant girls feel awful when they get dumped. One day they had a lover and the next they didn't.

Whether we like it or not, a girlfriend or wife must accept the fact that the other person is gone. Divorce has to be worse than death because both James and Daddy left voluntarily, but Theodore had no choice in the matter. Either way, the only thing the person left behind can do is to accept what happened. It's a miracle when two people stay together long enough to get married.

It hurt being rejected without knowing what I did or didn't do right. God, now that I know for myself how girls feel when they get dumped, please help me recognize playboys so I can, and will, know to avoid them.

Rosa Lee sat beside me without saying a word. Both her silence and her presence were priceless. She was wise to let my heart bleed without interruption.

Dang! Being in a relationship is a big deal. Nobody wants a broken heart, but some people don't care a bit about other people's feelings. Next time, my boyfriend will have to be my friend first.

Chapter 22

AFTER THE LAST DANCE

JAMES, MY FIRST LOVE, had become a stranger overnight without telling me what I'd done, or failed to do, to deserve being dumped. I had thought he was different from other athletes that got the big head when gullible girls went wild over them. But I was wrong.

I was very familiar with stories of backseat-of-the-car pregnancies and how boys would love girls and then leave them. Some of them ended up in shotgun weddings. I wanted to attract a boy like Cinderella did, not trap him like I was Captain Hook. No jock or anyone else was going to mess up my graduation plans if I could help it.

Not having a boyfriend didn't faze me until the Saturday evening I went to Elaine's house for the first weekly spring dance. Her mother was giving the dance to raise money for her son's graduation fees. Teenagers walked miles to converge on our neck of the woods.

There on Elaine's front porch was my brother, Harry, dancing all by himself like a professional entertainer. As Wilson Pickett's song "Do You Like Good Music?" played, the audience in the yard sang along and then screamed every time Harry spun around, slid across the slick concrete, and did the splits like James Brown. People waved both arms, tossed coins at his feet, and shouted, "Go Harry! Go head! You go boy!"

Harry's acrobatic moves were amazing. I felt proud to be his sister even though I had no idea that he could dance so well. Seeing my brother in a whole new light, made me realize that even people we think we know very well can surprise us. Harry the dancer! Who'd a thunk it! My lil' bro had found a fun way to earn money.

After his solo performance, Harry stooped down, swept up coins with both hands, stuffed them in his pockets, and headed home. Knowing that tightwad, he was going to count every penny and he wasn't going to tell Mama he had money 'cause she might want to borrow from him.

I thought about Harry while waiting in line to pay the ten cents admission to Elaine's living room. He'd learned the lesson Daddy taught us when he was very young: "Son, keep a jingle in your pocket. No girl want a broke man." Daddy was right. That's the reason why I'd mistreated Theodore at the prom.

Inside the huge living room, girls and boys stood along opposite walls checking each other out. Then s-l-o-w-l-y, one by one, the hawks moved in on their prey. Why did girls have to be treated like ripe plums waiting to be picked? I deserved to have fun after working that day and walking all the way home. It wasn't fair that girls should stand around waiting for a boy to ask us to dance. But to avoid giving the impression that I was fast, I waited until somebody noticed me.

Finally, a short, stocky guy that I had never seen before walked over to me and flashed a broad smile. One canine tooth glistened with gold. He stood out from the other boys because he had a thick mustache and wore a blood red shirt that made his skin look jet black.

"Cha Cha?" He extended his hand.

"Sure." I pushed through the wallflowers to get on the shellacked floor and stepped backward as he stepped forward. "One, two, cha, cha, cha."

Soon the floor was crowded and we had to dance closer together. One dance led to another, and then another. Pretty soon I realized that Alex had been my only dance partner all evening. He held me tight during a slow dance while Smokey Robinson and the Miracles sang, "You Really Got a Hold On Me." I felt safe in his arms.

After the last dance Alex and I talked as he walked me home. Without warning, he leaned over and kissed me goodnight under a full moon. He rubbed his bushy mustache around my mouth and then stuck his tongue inside. I felt the bumps on his tongue as it wiggled inside my mouth. My first kiss! I liked the tenderness of our lips pressed against each other but felt nervous about getting germs from his tongue sucking mine. I started to turn my head to pull away, but he grabbed my chin.

"I've got to go inside now," I lied. "My curfew is midnight."

Other girls had complained about having a curfew, but I made up my own because it seemed like it was a good thing to have.

"Well, ah, may I see you again next weekend?" he said, letting go of my chin.

"Sure. I'll be at Elaine's house next Saturday night. Goodnight."

He walked me to my front door and waited until I was safely inside before leaving. I liked that.

Who taught him how to French kiss? Who's supposed to teach kids how to kiss? I never saw Mama and Daddy do it. I did see my sister Lynette and Roscoe kiss at the drive-in when I was small, but I didn't know who taught them. Hmmm... I wonder who's supposed to teach children how to play husband and wife. Do people just naturally learn these things when they grow up?

Alex, a brick mason, was two years older and out of school. He had not graduated from high school but his job paid well and he had his own car. He wasn't a broke man. He showed up again the next Saturday night and we had a repeat of the previous week, including the goodnight kiss.

"I love you," he said.

"You don't even know me," I giggled.

"But I'm getting to know you. You're going to be my wife. May I come to visit you on Sunday afternoon around five?"

"Okay," I said.

Getting married was not on my list of things to do, but I liked the attention he gave me.

"What's your favorite flower?"

I hesitated, thinking of the ten-pound sack of flour in the grocery can, the orchid Theodore had given me, and roses in the garden.

"Bananas!"

He laughed. "All right, bananas it is."

I giggled, thinking, we could always use more food in our house.

Alex showed up with a big bunch of ripe Chiquita bananas on Sunday afternoon. I greeted him on the front porch. I had straightened up the living room before he arrived, but decided we'd have more privacy outdoors.

My little sisters ran outside to see who was coming to our house, but I shooed them back inside.

"Hey everybody, that's Alex. And he's coming to see me."

Mama came and peeked through the screen door. "Hey Alex," she said. "Did you meet Davida at her church?"

"No, Mama," I said, "We met at Elaine's house party."

"Oh. You seem like a nice boy."

"Thank you, ma'am," he said. "I try to be."

"Davida don't want a wolf in sheep's clothing," she said, and then disappeared.

Alex and I stared at each other.

"My mama likes to talk in riddles," I said, feeling a bit embarrassed.

"I understand. She wants you to be careful who you date."

That was the first of several Sunday afternoon visits at my house. As the weather got warmer and mosquitoes started biting me, I allowed Alex to come inside my house.

"I've always been ashamed to let anyone inside my house," I said.

"I didn't come to see your house. I came to see you."

"I'm glad." I was both flattered and delighted that somebody finally cared about me even though we were poor.

Most of the time I felt comfortable with him, but I told him Mama wouldn't let me ride in his car. That was to avoid having my own backseat-of-the-car story.

One afternoon, Alex scared the heck out of me after we listened to the Miracles sing "Shop Around." He jumped off the sofa, slapped his head and shook both fists, all because I'd said, "Girls should shop around just like boys." I truly believed that, but he disagreed. I froze on the spot. I wanted to push him out the door, but was too afraid to upset him more. He wasn't going to knock my teeth down my throat.

He calmed down and then sat on the sofa again.

"I'm so sorry," he said. "I didn't mean to scare you. I don't know why some things just make me sooo mad."

Ding! Ding! Ding! The uneasy feeling I had that day made me afraid to be alone with him. So, he became accustomed to my little sisters and brother and nephew hanging around. They loved having company as much as I did, especially when Alex brought enough bananas for each of them to get a whole one.

My constant reminders to Andrew and Yvette were, "Don't put your dirty hands on his pants. Find something to play with. Go color in your coloring books. He came to see me, not you." And each week I prayed, "Lord, don't let them upset him."

On the Saturday that I had gotten my first updo hairstyle, I felt as attractive as Elizabeth Taylor in Cat on a Hot Tin Roof. After debating with myself whether or not to go to the party, my heart turned a somersault when I stepped into Elaine's living room and saw Billy Sumter. What a surprise! Nobody knew I had a crush on this senior, a guy who never noticed me as he strolled through the school corridors on his long stilt-like legs. It was hard to keep my eyes off of him.

He stared at me from across the room and our eyes met.

"He sees me at last! Yes! Come on over," I thought.

It was amazing to see how a new hairdo could boost a girl's self-esteem. I'd considered not attending the dance that night, but decided to go and show off my hairstyle. Dancing was not part of the plan because I couldn't afford to sweat out my curls. My updo had to last until I took yearbook pictures on Monday morning. I wanted Alex to see how beautiful I looked before I slept on my hair.

Alex didn't show up, but Billy was there. Billy saw me standing along the wall and he saw me refuse dance offers as I waited for him to get the courage to approach me. The older women had taught us, "Ladies are supposed to be seen and not heard." It was up to the boy to take the initiative to get to know me better. So, I waited like a good girl.

Billy, with his cool pimp walk, finally stood in front of me with a big grin, "Can you spare a slice of gum?"

"I guess I got caught chewing with my mouth open." I giggled, and clumsily pulled a stick of Juicy Fruit out of the little party pouch hanging from my shoulder.

"Sorry, about the popping," I said, handing him the gum. "Students are supposed to know how to chew gum without getting caught by the teacher."

"You made it look so good, smacking your lips. I had to come and get some of what you've got."

We both laughed at the nuances in his statement. And for what seemed like hours, we stood there leaning against the wall, talking above the music and watching others dance.

"Enough talking," Billy said. "Let's dance."

"I thought you'd never ask." We pushed through the crowd onto the dance floor.

Billy twirled me around in a swing dance to the Temptations' "My Girl." He was handsome and a good dancer, the two characteristics Mama liked about Daddy. I felt like a princess whose knight in shining armor had finally found her. Much too soon after we began dancing, the dim blue party light went off and the bright white ceiling light came on.

"Good night ya'll," the disc jockey said.

"May I walk you home?" Billy said. He looked so bashful.

"I'd like that," I said.

A full moon brightened the road as Billy and I walked side-by-side in the middle of Cashmere Road toward my house at the bottom of the hill. We were laughing and talking about Harry's imitation of James Brown as the warm-up act when a car drove up behind us. Both of us stepped onto the dirt path alongside the pavement.

Instead of passing, the car pulled up beside us, too close for comfort.

I was walking a few steps ahead of Billy when I heard a familiar voice.

"Davida, is that your new boyfriend?" Alex asked from his seat behind the steering wheel.

"Keep walking," I said. Alex was trying to pick a fight.

He swerved the car like he intended to hit us.

Billy jumped out of the way, stopped, and said, "I know you've been seeing him, so I'm going to leave you two alone now. Goodnight." He turned and headed in the opposite direction.

Hurt, and furious enough to wish Alex dead, I walked faster while he drove close beside me. I refused to let him think I was scared of him. That was just what he wanted.

He blocked my way twice. The first time, I managed to squeeze between the front end of the car and the clay embankment of the country road. The second time, I walked behind the car and crossed over to the other side of Cashmere Road. Being on the opposite side of the driver made me feel a little safer. How I longed to get home. I just didn't want to run and make Alex think I was afraid.

"I want to know if that's your new boyfriend!" he shouted. His words exploded like the fizz from a shaken bottle of Pepsi that had just been opened.

I wanted to scream at him, but didn't have the courage to do so.

Suddenly, he swerved the car and blocked the path. I couldn't go forward because an embankment and a cow pasture with a barbed wire fence around it were beside me. If I ran around the car he could jump out and grab me.

"Get lost!" I yelled, feeling trapped, frightened, and annoyed.

"Do you want him or me?" he shouted.

"Him!" I yelled. I wanted my words to slash his throat. "You don't own me!"

Alex put the car in park and jumped out, leaving the driver's door open and the engine running.

I tried to run past him, but he yanked my arm. I pulled and kicked and swung my other arm at him. It seemed like I was pounding a brick wall with a feather.

Then he socked me in my forehead and I saw stars like those shown in cartoons when someone gets hit in the head. That one punch sent me careening backwards. I fell, rolled down a slope, and landed head first in a stream. I was stuck in the mud, unable to scream and unable to get up.

Bubbling water trickled into my ears as death closed in on me. Then I felt myself being lifted up. I gasped a couple of times. Death didn't get me after all.

Alex had snatched me out of the stream. He threw me over his shoulder like I was a croaker sack full of beans. Pinned down at the waist, I felt like a little child being carried up the hill, kicking and screaming. One foot felt lighter than the other, so I knew that one of my brown Penny Loafers was missing.

"I'm going to tell my mama to call the police on you!" I wiped mud away from my face and then remembered my plan not to mess up my hairdo. "Oh no!"

I don't believe this happened to me. I laughed and cried. This is insane!

Alex pushed me across the front seat past the steering wheel. Then, still clutching my arm, he hopped in and took off like he was driving a getaway car.

"I didn't mean to hit you like that! I mean it. I mean it. I didn't mean to hurt you!" He sounded confused, trying hard to convince himself rather than me.

"I never want to see you again," I sobbed. "You're going to pay for hitting me!"

Like a caged animal I clawed at the side of his face with my free arm while he held an ironclad grip on my left arm. I had no idea how far we'd traveled away from my house as we sped through country roads lined with black trees in the moonlight.

When the clock on the dashboard read one-thirty in the morning, I realized that he was not going to take me home until I calmed down. Wet, muddy and exhausted, I stopped crying and leaned back in the leather seat.

Alex drove sixty or seventy miles per hour to keep me from escaping. I regretted telling him about the time I jumped out of the toothless old man's car. Didn't he know I'd be crazy to jump out of a speeding vehicle with a madman I could see and land among snakes I couldn't see? Or maybe he was trying to find his way out of the back woods before he ran out of gas. Fear of making him angrier if I urinated on his seat made me squeeze to hold my pee.

God, please don't let him kill me. Make him take me home in one piece.

Without saying a word, Alex suddenly slowed down to fifty and then forty miles per hour. He also relaxed his grip on my wrist. Had God heard me?

It was almost two o'clock when he drove in front of my house and stopped.

"Get out," he grumbled, still staring at the road.

I popped out like a jack-in-the-box, slammed the door and dashed to the house just in case he changed his mind and came after me. Wearing only one shoe, I ran as fast as his car sped down Cashmere Road.

Home at last, I eased open the door and tiptoed across the living room, through the children's bedroom, and into the bathroom. That's where I flicked on the light to assess the damage.

"Oh, no!" I cried, seeing my muddy hairdo and a knot on my forehead. How can I look presentable on Monday? Why did I go to that dance? Why?

My love for Alex turned to hate as I stared at my gruesome image in the mirror. I was sorry I'd ever met him. I wanted to hurt him like he'd hurt me, but the safest thing to do was never to see him again. No jealous man was going to send me to an early grave. A woman would have to be crazy to marry or even date a man who would treat her like a punching bag.

I was combing mud out of my hair when Mama's reflection appeared in the mirror. She stood watching me.

What should I say? "I fell in a ditch," I mumbled.

Mama stared at me for a moment and then walked away. She knew I'd lied, but she didn't ask to hear more and I didn't offer.

After bathing and shampooing my hair, I cried myself to sleep. What had I done to deserve such a lousy night? What good is one shoe? Could I ever face Billy again? How embarrassing to get noticed and abandoned by the boy of my dreams in the same evening.

Sleep took forever to come. I turned from side to side wondering what had made me change my mind and go to the dance. I didn't have the time or money to get my hair done again. What a bummer! Mama's "follow your first mind" might be a true saying.

Before leaving for Sunday school, I brushed my hair in a ponytail and swirled shriveled bangs over the bruise on the side of my forehead. I put on a cute straw hat to hide my natural hair. My classmates were going to be surprised to see me wearing a hat over last night's beautiful hairdo, but I could tell them my hair got messed up while I slept.

We had an interesting lesson about Samson choosing the wrong girl. Elaine and I talked about her when we went to the restroom after class. While standing at the sink I took a quick look in the mirror to see if the knot on my forehead had gone down.

"What happened to that pretty hairdo you had last night?" she said.

"I had a fight with Alex and it got wet."

"He threw water on your hair?"

"Not exactly. He showed up after the last dance and got jealous when he saw Billy walking me home. And he... Well... He hit me."

"What! He hit you! Well, how did your hair get wet?

"I rolled down the hill and landed head first in the stream by my house. I never want to see him again as long as I live. From now on, please slap me if you see me talking to a knucklehead. Will you do that for me? No man will ever control me."

"Yeah! I'm with you! That sure looks like a painful lesson you learned." Remember, your Mama didn't give birth to a doormat!"

She touched the knot on my forehead.

"Ouch!" I pushed her hand away and smoothed down my bangs. Then we headed for the sanctuary.

"Don't ever date anybody with a hot temper and don't turn the other cheek," she said. "If you do he'll slap it, too. Just run, girlfriend. Run as fast as you can."

"You can bet I'll be more careful the next time I talk to a guy. Men flow in and out of your life like water, don't they?

"That's why you don't get attached 'til he puts a ring on your finger."

"Remember Samson broke up with that girl because he told an innocent little riddle that mushroomed. If I had dumped Alex as soon as I learned he had a short fuse he wouldn't have been able to beat up on me."

"Yeah, but it wasn't easy to get rid of him," she said. "You were scared to be alone with him and too scared to tell him to get lost. He wasn't the one for you."

"You're right. Two people who don't trust each other don't belong together. That's why my mama and daddy separated. I'm glad Samson learned that he couldn't trust that girl before they had children that would have to grow up without their daddy."

"I'm telling you, just because my daddy's at home doesn't mean everything is perfect," she said.

"Perfect? What's that? I ruined my chances with Billy, I wasted my money on a hairdo that got messed up, I broke up with a guy who thought he owned me, and tomorrow I'll take senior pictures with only-the-Lord-knows-what-type hairdo. I'm not looking for perfection. I'd settle for something good."

Rev. Taylor got my attention when he mentioned Samson. "Samson was furious about his bride betraying him, so he left her at the wedding feast and went back home to live with his parents. After he left, the bride's father gave her hand in marriage to the best man who happened to be on his post. Look, sometimes we try to make relationships work when they are doomed from the beginning. Don't settle for less than God's best for you. Samson was born to be a great leader but he chose not to listen to people who loved him. He was hardheaded, so God and his parents let him do whatever he wanted to do. Stay in the right path, children of God, and don't let nobody turn you 'round."

I leaned over and whispered to Elaine, "No knucklehead is going to stop me from being the first one in my family to graduate. I can, I will, I must. You'll see."

"Amen," she giggled.

Chapter 23
A SECOND CHANCE

ALEX DISAPPEARED. GOOD RIDDANCE was all I could say. That jealous knucklehead was not going to spoil my senior activities, especially the prom. I'd call the police if he ever came looking for a second chance to kill me. Why had I wasted my time with a man who made me feel uncomfortable?

Rehearsing for the senior class play, "The Phantom Strikes Again," kept me busy enough to forget about Alex, and yet made me jittery about the possibility of his crashing my prom. If he struck me once, he might try to hit me again. Some people need repeat lessons but I wasn't one of them. Never again would I let a man control my speech or my behavior.

One morning, three weeks before the deadline to submit the names of prom couples, I was standing in front of the school studying my lines for the play when Malachi, a smart boy in all my classes, approached me with a big grin.

"Davida, will you go to the prom with me," he blurted. His words sounded awkward, and they caught me by surprise like a sneak attack. I sensed that he had practiced them a hundred times.

I gazed into his brown eyes and saw that he was serious, yet afraid of hearing "no." Who would have guessed that he was shy?

"I hope nobody beat me to you," he said.

Wow! He expected competition.

"Yes. I'd love to go with you." It was hard resisting the urge to drop down on one knee and kiss his hand for saving me from the matchmaker this year.

"Whew! I'm glad I didn't wait too late," he said, grinning.

Malachi shook my hand hard like I was a dude. I'd never seen him so excited. Then he vanished.

Malachi was the date for me. *Pour moi?* He had tan skin with cat eyes—the kind that were brown during the day and gray at night. He was also polite, popular, and my close friend. I pinched my earlobe to ensure that I wasn't dreaming. I wondered if he could dance, but if not, he would still be a lot of fun.

Flabbergasted, I floated from class to class like a bubble drifting in a gentle breeze. The right guy knows how to make a slave girl feel like a princess. Memorizing lines was put on hold that day so I could savor Malachi's precious words. I couldn't have dreamed of a better prom date.

That evening on the phone, Elaine became the first to hear my good news.

"I'm going to have a great time at the prom this year," I said.

"What are you going to do that's so different from last year?"

"Well, first of all I'm going with my friend, Malachi. And I'll have a good attitude to make up for my mistakes with Theodore."

"Well all right then. Sounds good. I hope you enjoy this one."

"I know I will. I'm a changed person, thanks to Theodore."

***

After a successful class play, I made all arrangements for my prom. I didn't dare risk my date getting lost out in the country, so I planned to have Malachi pick me up downtown at mama's cousin's house. I barely knew Mrs. Smalls but I figured Mama was right when she said, "An ounce of prevention is worth more than a pound of cure."

Plus the change in location eased my fears of Alex doing something stupid to ruin my evening.

School ended at noon on the day of the prom. Many girls didn't show up for the half-day because hairdressers shampooed and made customers wait and wait, knowing they wouldn't leave with a nappy head. I'd already gotten my hair done, so I went to school because I wanted to earn my perfect attendance certificate.

That afternoon, I enjoyed a warm bubble bath and even soaked in the tub while home alone. After drying off, I rubbed Jergens lotion all over my body, rolled on an extra layer of Secret deodorant, sprayed Channel No. 5 on my chest, and patted dusting powder on my pubic hairs so there would be no foul odors. Then I stepped into my new nylon panties with a matching bra and put on blue jeans, a shirt, and a pair of flip-flops.

I opened the bathroom door to allow fragrances and steam to escape so the foggy mirror could clear up. After unwrapping the towel around my head, I saw my French roll intact even though it took forever before my swerved bangs lay flat. Then I brushed my teeth and tongue with Crest toothpaste and Arm & Hammer baking soda to be doubly sure I had no bad odors. I admired myself in the mirror, thinking about all the important things that are done in the smallest room in the house. I could tell people with an outhouse a thing or two about what they were missing by not having a bathroom.

My checklist came in handy as I packed a suitcase with my elbow length gloves, blue gown, and satin shoes from last year's prom. I added a new crinoline slip, pearl necklace and earrings, tiara, girdle, stockings, and satin purse containing lipstick, blush, eyebrow pencil, mascara, a round compact, and tiny plastic combination brush and comb.

The last thing I did was to paint my toenails and fingernails. It didn't make sense to bother when nobody would see them inside my shoes and gloves, but it seemed right to take care of the whole body.

I was still blowing my nails dry when Uncle Clyde pulled into the driveway. I'd promised him twenty dollars to pick me up on time and take me across town to Mr. and Mrs. Smalls' house on Rose Hill. We both knew that was big pay for two hours' work. I believed he would show up on time, and he did. His presence marked the beginning of a fantastic evening.

Grateful for my ride, I stepped out on the porch before Uncle Clyde could honk the horn. He sat behind the wheel with the engine running as I carried my suitcase toward his converted cab. Unlike my uncle who didn't offer to help me with my bag, I expected Malachi to do everything the teacher had taught in gentleman training sessions.

"Thank you for being on time," I said. "You're the best uncle in the whole wide world."

"I'm yo only uncle in town," he laughed.

"True." I put the suitcase on the backseat, and then sat in the front and handed him a twenty-dollar bill.

"Thank ya, thank ya," he said, tucking the money in his uniform shirt pocket.

"Mama arranged for me to spend the night on Rose Hill. I'll go to work from there tomorrow."

"Okay. Gotcha."

"You're better than a daddy to me."

"Whoooaa! David's still yo daddy. Nuthin'll ever change that. I just help out."

"I know. I know."

I couldn't help wondering what a real daddy would say to his daughter before she left for the prom with a boy he'd never met before. Would he put fear in her prom date so he would treat her like a lady? I wished I had some answers.

***

A little gray-haired lady stood looking through a big picture window when Uncle Clyde pulled in front of her paved, semi-circle driveway. Old Mrs. Smalls opened the front door of her brick house as soon as the car stopped.

"Hey you!" Uncle Clyde hollered.

"Hey yo'self," she said, waving at him from the front porch.

"Be back tomorrow!" He said, "I gotta get back to work."

I hopped out and grabbed my suitcase. He sped away right after I shut the door.

"Hello Mrs. Smalls," I said.

"C'mon in child. We's been specting ya. Ya shold look like yo mama."

"Thank you for letting me come over. This is a big help."

"Me and my husband glad to have ya. Glad to have ya."

In a vase next to the door was a vase full of red roses that both beautified the entrance and scented the house. I felt welcomed. What a perfect place to have Malachi pick me up.

I followed her to a bedroom at the end of a long hallway. In the room was a big bed covered with a colorful quilt, a wooden rocking chair with a plaid seat cover, a nightstand with a white, starched, crocheted tablecloth on it, and a floor-length mirror with a maple frame.

"It's so pretty in here," I said.

"Thank ya. This yo room for the night. Take yo time gittin dressed." She closed the door and left.

This is perfect! A house with a closet! Mama made a good choice.

I removed my gown from the suitcase and hung it in the closet just because I had one. Then I stood in front of the mirror and applied makeup. Getting my eyebrows perfect was hard work. After dressing, I practiced smiling and walking like Elizabeth Taylor in Butterfield 8. I wanted to look glamorous so Malachi would gawk at me.

Ding! Dong! The doorbell rang while I was twirling around in front of the mirror admiring myself for the twelfth time. The floor squeaked as slow-moving heavy footsteps passed my bedroom. The pitter-patter of lighter steps followed. I opened the door and saw Mr. Smalls headed for the front door with his wife at his heels. The way they did things together reminded me of my Grandpa and Grandma Cox when they were alive.

They were excited to have company. I took one final glance at myself in the mirror and then stepped into the hallway.

"C'mon in young man," Mr. Smalls thundered, pulling the wooden door wide open. He was a chubby man wearing bedroom slippers that looked much too big for his feet.

"Glad to make your acquaintance," Mrs. Smalls said. "Where you live?"

The tapping sound of my pumps on the hardwood floors captured their attention as I walked toward them. Mr. and Mrs. Smalls stepped to opposite sides of the narrow hallway and I got a glimpse of Malachi.

Malachi gaped at me. I flashed an Elizabeth Taylor smile and waited for him to speak.

"You look gorgeous!" He wolf-whistled.

"Thank you much," I nodded. "I welcome all compliments."

I stared at Malachi, dressed in his black tuxedo and royal blue bow tie and matching cummerbund.

"Don't you look handsome!"

"Thank you," he said, blushing.

In that moment I realized that boys enjoy compliments as much as girls.

"This is for you." He lifted my hand like a Don Juan and slipped a wrist corsage of white roses and royal blue ribbons onto my gloved arm. I felt like a princess.

Mr. and Mrs. Smalls clapped like they were watching a play.

"Ya done good!" Mrs. Smalls said in her squeaky voice, giggling.

"Dat's right, son," Mr. Smalls said. "Treat her like a lady."

"You all make me feel beautiful," I said, lifting the corsage to my nose and sniffing the fragrance. "Umm...Malachi, now it's my turn. Hold still while I pin this on you." On the first attempt, I pinned the white rose boutonniere on his lapel and patted it down.

"You look sharp as a tack, young man," Mr. Smalls said. "You two make a lovely couple. Now git her back here 'fo midnight. You can see we's old folks. We can't stay wake longer than twelve o'clock or we turn into grouchy old critters. So I needs to be sho dis girl is safe indoors befo we retire for da night."

Wow! My prom night daddy gave me a curfew. He had no idea how good it felt to have a man speak up for me.

"Sir, you have my word that I will have her back before midnight," Malachi said.

I was proud of Malachi, too, for talking man-to-man. He didn't sound shy at all.

Mr. Smalls turned on the porch light and then he and his wife stood in the doorway as we turned to leave.

Malachi stepped onto the porch and extended his hand to help me down the steps in my long gown. What a gentleman! He escorted me to the passenger side of his father's Buick and waited until I was comfortable before closing the door. He even tucked part of my dress inside. Once he settled behind the wheel, we waved goodbye to Mr. and Mrs. Smalls who stood on the front porch as we drove away.

"I like your grandparents," he said.

I remembered that I never introduced them, so he didn't know who they were. "I like them too," I giggled. I decided to leave well enough alone.

We talked about graduation and college on the short ride en route to our Tahitian Escapade at the Masonic Temple. It was a romantic atmosphere. Malachi and I mingled with other couples and danced and nibbled on hors d'oeuvres all evening. We stood in line laughing and talking with classmates as we waited to take the keepsake couple's prom picture. He purchased two pictures, one for himself and one for me. I was having the time of my life. I savored every moment and would have a picture to remind me of our perfect evening.

"This is how the prom is supposed to be," I said to myself as I we danced cheek to cheek to the soothing voice of Dionne Warwick's "I Say a Little Prayer for You." I was daydreaming in Malachi's arms and unaware that the music had stopped when he leaned back, stared at me with his eyes, now gray, and waved his hand in front of my face like it was a magic wand.

"Well, it's time to go now," he said.

I noticed that the shiny silver ball had stopped spinning and casting its glittering lights and the fluorescent lamps in the ceiling had come on. Everybody was leaving.

"Already?" I cooed, "It seems like we just got here."

"Stop acting silly. We've been here four hours. It's five past eleven." He took my hand and led me outside. It felt nice holding hands.

"Ahh," I sighed, inhaling fresh air. "Thank you so much for a wonderful evening."

"No! Thank you. I had a great time too. I didn't know you were so much fun outside of school. I think you could have stayed on the dance floor all night long."

"You're right."

The real test of whether or not he was a real gentleman was to see if he would be polite when the two of us were alone. He had passed the test. After making sure that I was comfortably seated in the car, he climbed behind the wheel and drove away.

"Aren't you going in the wrong direction?" I said.

"This is the way to Rose Hill," he said. He glanced over at me.

Then I remembered that he had not picked me up from home.

"Oh! I don't know what I was thinking about. I guess I'm still in Tahiti."

He laughed. "That was a great escapade while it lasted."

Malachi walked me to the door. I hugged him and pecked him on the cheek.

"Thank you for a great evening," he said.

The front door swung open and Mr. Smalls stood in the doorway.

"Thank you for gittin her back 'fo midnight young man. You a man of yo word. Good night."

I smiled at Malachi as I danced backward through the door behind Mr. Smalls. I felt valued, protected, respected and so glad to learn how it felt to be treated like a lady. I waltzed all the way down the hall to the guest room where I would spend the night resting on a bed of perfect prom memories.

Chapter 24
A BIG SURPRISE

AFTER MY PERFECT PROM I looked forward to graduation, the final and biggest senior event. I dreamed of seeing Mama and Daddy in the audience. In a few weeks, I would know if my dream had come true. An added bonus would be for them to shout out my name as I walk across the stage to receive my diploma.

Three weeks before graduation, the bus broke down and we arrived at school later than usual. I rushed to my locker but had to freeze when chimes from the PA system signaled the beginning of morning devotions. School rules required us to stop wherever we were out of respect for God while students prayed, read a Bible verse, and led the student body in reciting The Pledge of Allegiance.

A cheerful student voice came through the speakers as I stood at attention near the center of the long corridor near the main office. Across the hall stood Mr. Cannon, my guidance counselor. The chimes had caught his raised arm while he scratched his baldhead. He looked like he was posing for a photograph.

I stared at the floor to fight the giggles until the cheerful voice over the PA system said, "Have a good day!"

Mr. Cannon held out his raised hand, beckoned me with his fingers, and then went into his office.

What did I do? I plopped down in a wooden chair, thinking, he just wanted to play off his embarrassment at being caught with his hand in the air.

The secretary seated outside Mr. Cannon's private office pecked on the typewriter while I sulked about missing class. She was always typing.

Back in the fall, I'd spent hours in that office reading

college catalogues, studying for the Scholastic Aptitude Test, and completing applications for admission to MIT, Yale, Harvard, Princeton, and Waller College in Pennsylvania.

Mr. Cannon had been pleased that I'd selected four of the most prestigious colleges and universities in the United States. But my choices were based on getting as far away from Cashmere Road as possible. He had recommended Waller because that school was offering full four-year scholarships to minorities. "Waller is our safety school if the Ivy League schools don't come through with the financial aid we need." He and several other teachers had inspired me to maintain good citizenship, perfect attendance, and good grades so financial aid would not be a problem.

The entire college application process would have been overwhelming without his help. I was confident that I would be accepted when he assured me that my SAT mathematics score alone would attract attention.

Mr. Cannon opened his office door. I glanced at the wall clock and realized that I'd been waiting ten whole minutes.

"Come in, Davida," he said. I jumped up and rushed past him, trying to hide the fact that I was annoyed.

"Good morning. Have a seat," he said, closing the door.

"Morning sir," I mumbled as I plopped down in a leather chair. He loosened his necktie, then sat in the plush chair behind his desk and leaned back like he was stretching.

"Davida, I apologize for the wait. I've been preparing to talk to you."

I felt a knot in my stomach. Why did he have to prepare to talk to me? The serious look on his face made me nervous.

Don't tell me any bad news.

"You, young lady, have earned the second highest grade point average out of your entire graduating class of three hundred and sixty-six students." He whispered like he was afraid of being overheard. "Did you know that?"

"No, Sir." I wondered why he was being so secretive.

"Well, you should be very proud of your accomplishment," he said. "I know that there are some people in this school who do not want you to receive the honor you deserve. I even know who they are. Some people will not be pleased to hear that you qualify for class salutatorian. But, don't worry about them." He glanced down at a sheet of paper on his desk.

Is he saying this because I'm poor? I recalled him persuading me to let him take me home the night after dress rehearsal for the senior class play. Was he saying this because he'd seen my blockhouse in the country or because Mama told him something that time she came to speak to my teacher? Not knowing why people would be against me, I stared at him, wondering but daring not to ask, "What's a class salutatorian?"

"The class salutatorian is the student with the second highest grade point average in the school," he said. "That person delivers a speech at graduation."

"A speech?"

"Yes. You will need to prepare a speech and deliver it. Don't worry. I saw your performance in the senior class play. You were great. This morning I had you wait while I finished arranging help with your speech from an English teacher, Mrs. Drummer."

I tried in vain to grasp what he was really saying.

"This is a very special honor. You will address over a thousand people at the graduation ceremony. You must be sure to encourage your family to come to the Columbia Township Auditorium to support you."

Me? Deliver a speech to the whole school and parents, too. Me!

"What I've shared with you is strictly confidential. You must start preparing right away if you're going to deliver a polished salutatory in less than three weeks."

"Thank you, sir. I'm shocked." I shifted in my chair.

"It's great news! Remember, this is our secret. Share it only with your family."

Mr. Cannon scribbled his signature on a late pass to my first period English class and gave me a handwritten note telling my third period teacher to excuse me on Tuesday and Thursday of each week to meet with Mrs. Drummer.

I rushed to first period, slid into my seat, and opened my notebook. Mrs. Patterson stopped writing on the chalkboard. "Davida, do you have a tardy slip?"

The class snickered.

"Oh, yes ma'am. I'm sorry I forgot to put it on your desk." I ran and handed her my late pass.

"Awww, she would bring a note," a boy said.

As I returned to my seat, she said, "Davida knows what's required for success." The teacher paused and then returned to the lesson. "As I was saying, what are some other themes in Jane Eyre?"

I jotted the board notes in my personal version of shorthand: *impoverished Jane (imp J), wealthy, but tormented by Rochester (Roc), love and passion (l & p).* I wished I'd been present to hear Mrs. Patterson talk about love and passion. Second-hand notes from classmates never compare with getting lessons straight from the teacher's mouth.

Concentrating on schoolwork that day was difficult. Mr. Cannon's requirement that I keep our secret made me feel like I had lockjaw. All my hard work had paid off in a big way, but I couldn't tell anybody.

While walking to work after school, I imagined being Mary Magdalene on her way to tell Jesus' disciples that she had seen the risen Lord. Perhaps she worried that people wouldn't believe that she, of all people, had the honor of being the first person to see Jesus after he arose from the dead. That must have been a gigantic pill for her to swallow. Out of all the students in my class, who would believe that a garbage man's daughter was going to speak at graduation? Unbelievable!

Instead of my professional smile, mine was genuine that night as I walked around in the Toy Department. Life was good to me. Real good.

After work, I burst through the front door telling Mama, "You have to come to my graduation and hear my speech. Mr. Cannon said, 'Your parents have got to come and support you.' "

She stared at me from her sewing machine like I had lost my mind.

Of course, my counselor didn't know that Mama only finished sixth grade and Daddy dropped out in fifth. That was my business. He didn't realize that graduation was an opportunity to get Mama and Daddy together in the same room. They hadn't seen each other since I was in third grade. I imagined them falling in love again, and getting back together.

My Mama's blank stare made me realize that I'd have to do more than tell her she had to come to my graduation.

***

On Tuesday, I went to see Mrs. Drummer, the English teacher, who had been assigned to help me write my speech.

"You write the first draft of the speech and bring it to me on Thursday and we'll go from there," she said.

Clueless as to what my speech should contain, I stopped by the library and looked up the word salutatory in Webster's Dictionary. I read, "an address of welcome, esp. one given as an oration by the student ranking second highest in a graduating class at a high school or college."

I thought of church members welcoming visitors at Corinthian Baptist. They often said a few words before saying, "We welcome you once, we welcome you twice, we welcome you in the name of Jesus Christ. Welcome, welcome, welcome." So, I scribbled my initial draft, and made it brief and concise like the church greeting.

I wrote:

"Ladies and gentlemen, this is the day we've worked toward for twelve long years. We've come through many teachers, subjects, sleepless nights, and salty tears. We thank each and every one of you who came out to support us tonight, and our prayer is that you'll enjoy this occasion as you observe the brightest of the bright, who earned the right, to appear on this platform in the spotlight. On behalf of the class of 1966, I welcome you."

On Thursday I read my speech to Mrs. Drummer. "Hmmmm," she said.

She was not pleased. I wanted to say, "Just give me the bad news, then help me do it right." But, I watched and waited.

Mrs. Drummer closed her eyes, propped both elbows on her desk, clasped her hands together to form a triangle, and leaned her forehead against them.

What was she thinking? My goodness! If writing a welcome speech baffled the second smartest student in the school, then she must want something special.

"Your speech is nice," she said, raising her head. "But it lacks depth." She stared at pictures of Gwendolyn Brooks and James Baldwin on the bulletin board. Then she removed a pencil from behind her right ear and stroked her pressed hair on one side. After a minute or two her gaze went through my eyes and into my soul. She seemed to have gotten a revelation from God.

"This is a pivotal time in our country's history," she said. "Last year we witnessed the mandatory desegregation of public colleges. Public schools are next. As a matter of fact, I know you would have been denied the honor of being selected class salutatorian had you transferred to the school nearest you at the beginning of this school year. Separate but equal is a lie when it comes to quality education. I don't know exactly what the future has in

store for our students or even Negro teachers, but I do
know that your speech must emphasize that a changing
of the guard is imminent. Give me a few days and I'll get
back to you with ideas for your speech."

"Yes, ma'am." I really didn't understand what she
was saying but it was quite obvious that the speech was
more important than I could even imagine.

The following Tuesday, at our third meeting, Mrs.
Drummer handed me a three-page typed speech. I read
it aloud and was overwhelmed by the length and the
verbiage. I would never have thought of those things even
if Langston Hughes had been my brother or Dr. Martin
Luther King, Jr., my father.

"Read it several times and come back on Thursday
prepared to read it aloud," she said.

So this is a salutatory!

"Work on memorizing one paragraph at a time," she
said. "I want to see progress when we meet again. Practice
reciting the whole speech every day until graduation."

"Yes, ma'am." The teacher had done my assignment.
This must be important!

Clutching the priceless pages, I left the classroom
wondering why Mrs. Drummer hadn't bothered to help
me write my own speech. Did she think I was incapable
of doing a fine job with her help? Then a positive
thought followed the negative one. Maybe she wanted
to expedite the preparation phase in order to concentrate
on the execution phase since we only have a couple of
weeks left.

I liked the speech Mrs. Drummer had given me. I
thanked God for it and prayed, "Please help me memorize
it." This is bigger than the senior class play. It's my big
chance to show everybody how well I can perform solo.

Over and over again, I recited my speech silently on
the school bus ride home. My family was the first live
audience to see the hand gestures that I added to make my
words come alive. They clapped and cheered, and boosted
my confidence. Whenever I missed a word, Vera stopped

me. Pretty soon, even my youngest sisters could tell me when I omitted a word.

Mrs. Drummer was ecstatic when I read to her that first Thursday.

"Bravo! Bravo! There's nothing wrong with reciting a speech that you did not write yourself," she said. "Mr. Cannon's daughter is the valedictorian. I assure you that he will help her write her valedictory, which is the farewell address. You're off to a great start. Just continue memorizing it and you will do a fantastic job!"

She made it seem like the salutatorian was competing with the valedictorian. It didn't make sense because the purpose of each speech was different. A welcome and a farewell are like two bookends with plenty in the middle to keep them separated.

I went to the library and looked up some of the words in my speech to get a better understanding of what I was saying. I found them in "Days," a poem by Ralph Waldo Emerson, who died in 1882; "To Think of Time" by Walt Whitman, who died in 1892; and a quote by Johann Wolfgang von Goethe, a famous German author, who died in 1832. How Interesting! Like prophets in the Bible, they had predicted what people would go through in 1966.

Persuading Mama and Daddy to come to my graduation was much harder than learning my speech. Although I was frustrated, I continued to drop reminders and remained optimistic.

"What are they going to do?" Mama said. "Why do you need me there? Can't you say your speech without me? Will I have to say sum'in? How do I need to dress? How long will it take? Do we have to stay 'til it's over? Will I have to stand in front of people? Do we have to pay to get in? Will we have tickets? Will they have special seats for us? Who all will be there?"

Her questions made sense. I just couldn't answer them. It was my first graduation too.

I called Daddy's job and asked his boss to urge him to come to my graduation. Daddy returned my call and asked: "What's a graduation? How much will it cost to get in? Do I need to dress up? Who all will be there? How will I find you 'mongst all them people? What are they going to do there? Will they let a garbage man come in? Do I have to take the day off work? Do I have to bring something? Do you need me and yo Mama there?"

"Daddy, I can't answer all your questions, but my counselor said you need to be there," I said. "So, please come. Pleeeease hear my heart and not just my words."

I hung up the phone. "Both my parents are coming to my high school graduation! I don't know how to get them there, but they will come in Jesus' name." I declared it to encourage myself as tears crawled out of my eyes.

I prayed harder than I'd ever done before in my life. I knew my parents couldn't come along with me because I had to report early and I needed to concentrate on my speech. So I asked Uncle Clyde to bring Mama, and Miss Annie Mae (Daddy's pop-eyed girlfriend) to make him come to the auditorium. Before long, I would know if my prayer had been answered. Maybe, just maybe, when they see each other again after nine years they'll remember that they're still married. They separated but never divorced, so I had a reason to hope that the two lovers would be reunited.

I requested two tickets for my parents to sit in front row seats 103 and 104 at the Columbia Township Auditorium. The best graduation gift I could get would be to look into the audience and see Mama and Daddy seated side by side.

Chapter 25
RETROSPECT, PROSPECT

ACCORDING TO THE NEON SIGN IN FRONT of the Columbia Township Auditorium, we, the Class of 1966, were tonight's special attraction. Being a celebrity felt real good.

So this is graduation! All the preparation was worth that moment when ushers pushed open the side entrance double doors. The crowd roared as the processional began. Two-by-two, green caps and gowns flowed into the Columbia Township Auditorium like waves descending on a beach. Some graduates marched to their seats in the band, others to the chorale, and the rest to reserved seating on the podium.

I fought back the urge to shout when I spotted Mama and Daddy seated side-by-side in the first row. A shockwave went through me from head to toe as though I'd been struck by a lightning bolt. They looked beautiful together. All my hard work had paid off. I felt like shouting, but I dared not break stride.

Will they get back together?

Daddy spotted me wearing my gold honor sash as I marched behind Mr. Cannon to the tune of Pomp and Circumstance played by our band. He tapped Mama's arm and pointed to me. She waved.

Smiling, I blew her a kiss, but kept moving toward my assigned seat on the podium. I didn't even realize my cheeks were wet until Mrs. Drummer leaned forward and handed me a tissue.

"You'll do just fine!" she whispered.

She had no idea how many years I'd yearned to see my parents together. All the years of longing ended on my graduation day. My biggest wish had come true.

Thank God the principal and the chorale were on program ahead of me. I needed time to pull myself together. So I took several deep breaths while waiting to stand and deliver my salutatory.

I couldn't remember if I should acknowledge my parents' presence. "Help me Jesus?" I prayed. "You speak through me 'cause I can't even think straight right now."

Following the opening remarks by the principal, the Madison Chorale set the atmosphere with a superb rendition of "His Eye Is On the Sparrow."

"God, you see me. You see me. You know I need you."

Then, taking one last deep breath, I rose from my seat on the podium and stepped to the lectern. My gold tassel dangled from the right side of my cap as a reminder that graduation was now in progress.

This is it! I was confident that my speech would make my parents proud. I knew exactly where, when, and how to interject gestures and intonations for a polished delivery. After adjusting the microphone to my height, I allowed the following words to flow through my lips, determined to leave an indelible impression on people's minds:

"Retrospect, Prospect.
Daughters of Time, the hypocritic Days,
Muffled and dumb like barefoot dervishes,
And marching single in an endless file,
Bring diadems and fagots in their hands.
To each they offer gifts after his will,
Bread, Kingdoms, stars and sky that holds them all.
I, in my pleached garden, watching the pomp,
Forgot my morning wishes, hastily
Took a few herbs and apples, and the Day
Turned and departed silent. I, too, late,
Under her solemn fillet saw the scorn.

"It is not unwitting, as one moves from one scene of life to another, to consider carefully his potentials and inadequacies, to assess without preconceived bias the path he has chosen to follow. What paths have we advisedly or inadvisably chosen to savor? Of what substance and character have the fruits of life been that we have so arduously partaken? Has this phase of our life's plan been inadvertently perceived or rather pursued with calculated, responsible solicitude? Too, too often, as Ralph Waldo Emerson suggests, we have only taken 'a few herbs and apples' and 'too late,' have amassed the wisdom to discern our folly.

"We, each of us, have been offered gifts of immeasurable value. We have accepted them as only our limited knowledge, abilities, desires, objectives, and experiences have dictated. In far too many instances, we have been found 'watching the pomp' and allowing it to pass us by, 'forgetting our morning wishes' and permitting the 'day to turn and depart silently away.'

"Ours have been lives steeped with insufficient preparation, inadequate moral and ethical standards, social and economic inequities, inoperative judgment, and personal problems which have been nearly chaotic in their effect upon us. Far too many of us have not adequately incorporated within our perspective the discipline unselfishly offered in our earlier years by our devoted parents, nor the wisdom permeated in our later years by those dedicated to instruct. The loss has been solely ours. This has been in reality a criminal act perpetrated by abortive vision.

"But to bathe in the sorrow of our past is to lie dormant. Of this we must not, we must not be adjudged guilty. This complex and ever-demanding society of which we are a part, rarely grants us the opportunity of revel in empty splendor without penalty. It is now that we must engage in objective introspection. We should assess our encumbrances and regard them as expensive learning experiences. We should ascertain our assets and strive to compliment them. We should make use of those talents and worthy traits immediately evident that we possess. We should discover those desirable hidden qualities with which we have been endowed and put forth serious effort to enhance them. We should embark upon a new course, designed to provide for us, in its pursuit and termination, a rewarding life. Johann Wolfgang von Goethe aptly stated, 'I find the great thing in the world is not so much where we stand, as in what direction we are moving.' Such is the challenge we face as we begin a new act in our lives.

"The world we enter will not greet us with outstretched arms, as a mother receives her newly born child. Recently conceived opportunities are ours to realize only if we earn the right to demand and receive them. No longer will our extenuations be tolerated. Our cries of 'foul' will more certainly fall upon deaf ears and our failures shall remain inexplicable.

"In treading more clearly perceived paths, we must maintain our self-respect, liberate ourselves from that which ties us to the past, emancipate ourselves from the tentacles of habitual lack of preparedness, reconstitute our values and attitudes, and subordinate immediate levity to long-range goals. The members of the Class of 1966 have the courage, the stamina and the zeal to accept the demanding call of today to make secure the future of tomorrow.

In the subtle words of Walt Whitman, 'The law of the past cannot be eluded; the law of the present and the future cannot be eluded...'

"Loved ones, ladies and gentlemen, with this graduation ceremony tonight, we have reached the first significant milestone in our lives. Your presence and assurance of good wishes for our future success shall always be remembered fondly. The Class of 1966 welcomes you and is delighted to have you share this experience with us.

Thank you."

The audience of more than a thousand, including my mama and daddy, gave me a thunderous applause and a standing ovation. My parents beamed with pride, even if they didn't understand a word of what I'd said. I felt special, loved, and successful. Their presence meant more than the diploma I would receive that night.

Returning to my seat, I saw all thirty-two of Mrs. Drummer's teeth. Practice does make perfect. That speech was a piece of cake! All I needed to know was what to say, when to say it, how to say it, and where to interject gestures. Public speaking was fun. Words, when released with energy and passion, have the power to penetrate the hardest head or hardest heart.

Did anybody have an inkling that a little nobody like me could rise above my circumstances? Perhaps God put me in a poor family to show the world that ordinary children of school dropouts can do extraordinary things. Now, anybody who thought that I didn't deserve the privilege of addressing tonight's crowd could see how wrong they were. This daughter of a hotel maid and a garbage man had something important to say.

Mr. Cannon headed to the microphone as I returned to my seat.

"Davida, come back," he said into the microphone.

I turned and went back to the lectern. Mr. Cannon gestured for me to stand beside him. The audience continued to clap. Seeing Daddy wave both fists in the air blurred my vision. He looked like Muhammad Ali standing in the ring cheering for himself after knocking out his opponent. Was he celebrating himself or me?

Mr. Cannon waited for the applause to die down. Then he stared at me and spoke.

"It is my pleasure to announce that this young lady, Davida Kincaid, is the recipient of a full four-year scholarship to Waller College in Pennsylvania."

"Really! I am?"

He nodded. "Yes, you are."

"Yippee!" I must have jumped three feet off the floor.

When I landed, I tap danced and shook both fists in the air like my daddy had done. Still trying to grasp the meaning of his words, I cried, "I'm going away to college!"

More clapping ensued.

My body sat back down, but my mind wandered around in Pennsylvania until Mr. Cannon announced that Madison High's Chorale was next.

"Following the musical selection, our next speaker will deliver the valedictory, the farewell address delivered by the student with the highest academic achievements. I am delighted to have the honor of introducing this year's valedictorian. Erika Cannon, a young lady who ranks number one in both my personal and professional life, will speak after this selection."

"Ahhh," seniors on the platform said in unison.

Wow! Some people have everything.

Mr. Cannon nodded at the choir director. Madison's Chorale sang "Victory In Jesus" by Eugene M. Bartlett. The singing was incredibly good! The audience clapped like we were in a Sunday morning church service.

After the Chorale's immaculate performance, Mr. Cannon walked over and escorted his only daughter to the lectern.

Erika was tall and thin, the spitting image of her father and the same height, too. She floated to the lectern barely touching the crook in his arm. He handled her like she was precious china. Her facial expression exuded confidence. She held her head high like she deserved to be treated like a princess. It was obvious that they had practiced for that moment.

When they reached the lectern, Mr. Cannon placed his hands together and bowed to her like he was saying a good night prayer. She curtsied and watched him leave as he returned to his seat on the podium.

"Ahhhh..." The audience responded with loud clapping.

She is sooo fortunate. While Erika delivered her valedictory, I thought about how proud she'd made her parents. Mrs. Drummer was right. Mr. Cannon helped his daughter with her speech because it, too, contained words I'd never heard before. My ears perked up when she mentioned "zoot suits."

"Zoot suits?" echoed the audience.

I smiled. They were listening.

Hmm... They must have been totally lost when I recited my speech. I only said what I'd been taught, including words I didn't understand. Even though I delivered a dynamic speech, my understanding of our changing times was no better than that of my classmates. Desegregation had people asking, "What's going on?" Integration required Negroes to be bussed to all white schools. Why weren't white students bussed to Madison? Integration put a bad taste in my mouth because it started off not being fair.

Applause from the audience interrupted my thoughts. Erika had finished her speech and was receiving her standing ovation. I jumped up as Mr. Cannon ran over and hugged her.

The "zoot suits" had made me miss the remainder of Erika's speech. Oh well.

Graduates started fidgeting. It was time for the best part of the program—presentations. Showtime had come. After each name was announced, that person had a moment to get everybody's attention. After strutting our stuff we would be rewarded with a fake diploma to be exchanged for the real one tomorrow.

The only name I listened for was "Davida Kincaid." No one else mattered even though I laughed a lot before the K's were reached. What a delicious taste of victory to cross the finish line after twelve long years. Whew! I made it. I'll walk for Theodore, too.

After switching tassels from the right to the left side of our caps, the graduates were as antsy. The closing song, our Alma Mater, was barely finished when caps flew into the air and pandemonium broke out. It sounded like everybody was screaming and crying. I couldn't stop shouting, "I did it! I did it!"

What a celebration!

Daddy pushed through the crowd and hugged me before I left the podium. His alcohol or pride announced, "I'm David Kincaid, and this here's my daughter, Davida Kincaid. Mark my words, this garbage man's daughter is going somewhere in this life."

Did he get jealous of Mr. Cannon for being on stage with Erika?

Daddy's speech reminded me of all the Sunday afternoon stories he used to tell us when we all lived together. Will he tell Miss Annie Mae's children my graduation story? The thought made me sick to my stomach. I walked toward the exit behind Mama and Uncle Clyde with Daddy right beside me, except for the two times when he swayed a bit.

Mr. Cannon proved to be a good man. He made sure that I wasn't cheated out of being class salutatorian. Though my counselor, he acted like a father fighting for his child. What does a person have to do to become a daddy like that? How does a child get to have a daddy like that?

"See ya'll later," Daddy said, when we stepped outside into the night air.

One moment I glimpsed him and the next all I could see was his Stetson hat bobbing above a throng of people all around him. He turned left while we went right. My matchmaker plan hadn't worked, but I wasn't sorry for trying.

"Goodnight," I mumbled, looking in his direction.

Glancing up at the night sky speckled with thousands of stars, I reminded myself that I had done my job of bringing Daddy and Mama together one more time. I felt loved and supported when I looked into the audience and saw my parents seated out there. What an unforgettable experience!

As Uncle Clyde drove away from the Columbia Township Auditorium where I'd gotten my first taste of celebrity status, I stared at the dispersing crowd and wondered if other graduates felt equally ready and able to conquer whatever the future had in store for us. I was thinking about my scholarship and what I had to do to keep the money so I could stay in college, when Mama broke the silence.

"That's the first time I seen David since we separated," she said. "He looks good. Sittin' side him tonight was the longest we ever been together in one room without fightin'. I don't miss him one bit."

"Ya right, he do look good," Uncle Clyde said. "I was wondring if ya'll was gonna try it again."

"Nope," she said. "I'm good just like I is. Just need mo money. That's all."

Neither Daddy nor Mama wanted to get back together. They both had put nails in the marriage coffin. Now, all they needed to do was bury it. In one way I was sorry their love hadn't been rekindled. But in another way, I wasn't. So much had happened since they broke up.

***

The next morning, I went back to school to pick up my official high school diploma.

"Davida, you did a superb job of presenting that speech last night," Mr. Smith, my homeroom teacher, said.

"Thank you, Sir."

"I could tell you didn't write it," he said. "And I even know who did."

Not knowing exactly how to respond, I just listened. Did he like the speech?

He thumbed through the stack of diplomas on his desk, stopped at mine and handed it to me without looking up, and said, "Have a good life."

I stepped aside when Mr. Smith glanced at the next student in line and began searching for his diploma.

My feelings were hurt as I left the classroom befuddled. What was Mr. Smith's point? I didn't get it.

Was he saying that he would have preferred to hear a speech that I had written? Was he one of those who didn't want me to be salutatorian? Had he hurt Mrs. Drummer's feelings too?

"Trying to figure out these adult relationships racks my brain!" I mumbled. "It sure is funny how one moment a person can lift you up and then the next moment that same person can tear you down with WORDS. Whoever said, 'Sticks and stones may break my bones but words will never hurt me' lied. Words can cut a person in half like a sword."

Daddy had come to graduation and talked like he was so proud of me. He acted like he'd forgotten telling me, "You my daughter. At least yo mama say ya is." He didn't have a clue how much those words hurt. Oh well, it doesn't matter now. In spite of his words, or because of them, I'm going away to college.

I strolled down the corridor toward the exit doors of Madison High for the last time, smiling at the thought of leaving my school, my house, and Columbia. I looked up and noticed painted messages on the walls that had been there all three years but I'd never paid attention to them before.

In bold black manuscript I read, **"Much is required from the person to whom much is given"** (Luke 12:48). I thought, "That means I had to go through everything I endured to gain the strength, courage, confidence and great joy I have today. God has given me wisdom, knowledge, understanding, and abilities that I must share with other people."

Next, written in cursive, was *"So the last shall be first, and the first last"* (Matthew 20:16). I giggled. I thought, "That's me. It's hard to win the victory when you have a late or rough start. I'm so glad I refused to become discouraged by my circumstances. There was no way I could ever give up on my dreams. I thank God for all of my teachers, both inside and outside the classroom, because each one encouraged me in some unique way to come from behind, catch up, and move to the front of the class. And I did."

Above the exit doors were huge letters in calligraphy: *"The end of a thing is better than its beginning; the patient in spirit is better than the proud in spirit"* (Ecclesiastes 7:8). "I know that's true now that I've walked the stage," I whispered. The walls were talking to me.

I lifted the padded green and gold leather jacket containing my diploma to my lips, kissed it and waved it at God.

"Thank you for this piece of paper that holds the key to my future. This is my ticket out of the country. Ha! Ha! Ha!"

During those times when I was weak and on the verge of giving up or giving in, God stepped in and showed me his power to do great things in me, for me, and through me. He used me, and my shameful life, to encourage other people to keep their focus on Him instead of their circumstances. I was a walking miracle.

"Now I get it! As James Brown said, 'I feel good! So good! I've got you!' "

I ran down the stairs and out the exit toward my school bus. In the Carolina sunshine, a powerful sense of victory enveloped me. Clutching my diploma like it was a marathon winner's prized trophy, I raised both arms and saluted my future.

Resisting the urge to glance back, I shouted, "Look out Waller College! Here comes the garbage man's daughter!"

EPILOGUE

LETTING GO OF SCARS concludes The Garbage Man's Daughter series. What a tearful journey! Many of the issues addressed in these books have not changed in half a century. Therefore, Davida Kincaid's story reminds us of the need to repent of sexual immorality, to cease making ostentatious claims of being Christian, and to revise unjust laws that undermine the marriage covenant and destroys the family.

Children yearn for family unity, acceptance, love, and security in a stable environment. They learn what they live, and without proper intervention, live what they learn. At every stage in Davida's development she acknowledges a teacher for impacting her life in either a positive or negative way.

Davida represents just one of many children whose world has been shattered and redirected by separation and divorce. Children of divorced parents often suffer shame and poor health, perform and behave poorly in school, blame themselves for the family breakdown, turn to gangs, drugs, alcohol, sexual promiscuity, violence, and sometimes suicide. They often have trouble forming and keeping stable relationships and perceive the world through lenses tinted by their own experiences. Both letting go of hope for restoration of the family unit and adjusting to life in a single-parent home can be challenging for all, even when separation ends domestic violence.

Let's preserve the institution of marriage and give our progeny hope for the future. We can by remembering that God, the real garbage man in this series, is willing to relieve us of rubbish in our lives. Trust is demonstrated by letting go of everything that hinders a personal relationship with Him and with others. Going a step beyond the earthly garbageman who takes away only those things we release, 1 Peter 5:7 says "Give *all* your worries and cares to God, for he cares about you." We are also given assurance in Psalm 103:12 that "He has removed our sins as far from us as the east is from the west."

Can you imagine all clutter being removed from your house? Talking about shame, secrets, stress, and scars that you've been holding onto is quite therapeutic.

Thank you for taking this liberating journey with Davida.

CHAPTER QUESTIONS
FOR SELF REFLECTION

1. Give an example of a happy family. Explain.
2. Why would a person spend more money on alcohol than on food?
3. Who taught you how to manage your money? Your time?
4. What activities do you and your father and/or mother regularly do together?
5. Describe one of your most memorable experiences? Why that one?
6. What are your priorities? What would make you change them?
7. What scars are you covering up? What would make you open up?
8. What has been a major disappointment for you? What did you learn from it?
9. What are some responsibilities that children should not be assigned?
10. Under what circumstances is a parent justified in giving away a child?
11. Who teaches a child how to perceive the other woman or man after the family breakup?
12. How do you handle negative truth(s) about your daddy? Your mama?
13. How faithful are you in keeping your promises? Why?
14. Why do some people perceive dark skin as inferior? What's your view?
15. With whom do you share the pain of your emotional scars? Why that person?
16. Describe an occasion when you were the honoree or treated very special.

17. On what issue would you dare to differ from the majority?
18. Describe an ongoing personal challenge. Why do you struggle with it?
19. How do you respond when you know you've been treated unfairly?
20. What big blunder have you made that you'd like to forget?
21. Describe the attraction between you and your first boyfriend or girlfriend.
22. What would make you stay in an abusive relationship? Explain.
23. Who trains a boy/girl to behave like a gentleman/lady?
24. What or who is given credit for your success? What words would you say to people who said you would not succeed?
25. What is your dream goal? What will you say when the dream comes true?

ABOUT THE AUTHOR

GLORIA SHELL MITCHELL, DMin (Davida Kincaid in *The Garbage Man's Daughter Series*) is a minister, educator, divorce researcher and radio talk show host on KTYM.com, wilkinsradio.com and rmcgospel.com.

Since her first published piece, a letter to the editor of *Ebony Magazine* at age 12, her articles have been published in Literary Landscapes, Event Magazine, gospelroads. com, patch.com, Bukisa.com, and *Testamentum Imperium* An International Theological Journal in which "The Importance of Grace in Compassionately Addressing Divorce" appears. In addition to her published dissertation *Compassionately Addressing Divorce: A Redemptive Model of Ministry to Divorced Christian Leaders,* she has authored three self-published books in *The Garbage Man's Daughter Series: Letting Go of Shame* (Book 1); *Letting Go of SECRETS* (Book 2); *Letting Go of STRESS* (Book 3). She is currently writing Kiss Shame Goodbye, a memoir about Davida's tumultuous marriage to her high school sweetheart.

Although written from a child's perspective, *The Garbage Man's Daughter Series* is based on years of research and personal experience as a teacher, child of divorce, a divorcee, and facilitator of divorce support groups.

Gloria has two daughters, Richette and Joy, and lives in Southern California.

www.ingramcontent.com/pod-product-compliance
Lightning Source LLC
Chambersburg PA
CBHW071525040426
42452CB00008B/896